The STORM before the CALM

NEALE DONALD WALSCH

A New Human Manifesto

The STORM

before the CALM

Book 1 in the
CONVERSATIONS WITH HUMANITY
Series

an *EmNin* book

Published in the United States by: Emnin Books, 324 Wimer St.,
Ashland, OR 97520 • emninbooks@aol.com

Distributed in the United States by: Hay House, Inc.: www.hayhouse.com®

Published and distributed in Australia by: Hay House Australia Pty. Ltd.:
www.hayhouse.com.au • *Published and distributed in the United Kingdom by:* Hay House UK, Ltd.:
www.hayhouse.co.uk • *Published and distributed in the Republic of South Africa by:* Hay House
SA (Pty), Ltd.: www.hayhouse.co.za • *Distributed in Canada by:* Raincoast: www.raincoast.com •
Published in India by: Hay House Publishers India: www.hayhouse.co.in

Cover and interior design by: Frame25 Productions
Cover photo: © James Thew, c/o Shutterstock.com

Library of Congress Control Number: 2011926301

ISBN: 978-1-4019-3692-1
Digital ISBN: 978-1-4019-3693-8

14 13 12 11   5 4 3 2
1st edition, October 2011
2nd edition, October 2011

Printed in the United States of America

*If you could have a loving, caring conversation
with humanity at this challenging and
frightening time, and if you knew that
people would listen, what would you say?*

PART ONE

Ending the Fear, Starting the Adventure

The world is changing
and it's not what it seems

CAN WE TALK?

MY DEAR, DEAR FRIENDS...my wonderful companions on this human journey...

I'm so glad that you're here, and I hope that your answer to the question just above is yes, because it's very important that you hear this: We're experiencing something quite extraordinary on the earth right now. I'm going to give it a name here.

We are experiencing The Overhaul of Humanity.

This is not an exaggeration. This is reality. It is observable at every turn.

Yet here is something that is not so observable: *Things are not as they seem.*

And I think, before the world and its people get too far along this road, we all need to be aware of that.

We also need to be aware that there's nothing to be afraid of in our future if we will all but play our role in creating it. And that role—the role we are being invited to play by Life Itself—is going to be very *easy* to play.

I have more that I want to share with you around all this. Let me give you a summary of everything I have come here to say:

- A major shift is occurring on our planet.

- There is nothing to be afraid of if we all play our role in this shift.

- Our role is easy to play, and it can actually be fun.

- It involves having fabulous conversations revolving around seven simple questions.

- The asking and answering of these questions can result in the creating of solutions to humanity's biggest problems.

- It is time for us to place before humanity a New Cultural Story, sending us in brand new directions in politics, economics, culture, education, relationships, work, marriage, sexuality, parenting, and every area of human endeavor; a manifesto created by all of us, working as co-authors.

- There are some exciting opening thoughts about what that document could contain that I think you should hear.

Oh, and I don't want to talk with you just about "world conditions" or "the global situation" or "our planetary crisis." As important as those topics are, I'm clear that the Overhaul of Humanity is overhauling each of us. One look at how much has changed in *your* life in the past three years will tell you that.

So I'd like to have some exchanges with you as well about easing any struggle or negativity that may be present in your own personal life.

Okay, there you have it. The whole agenda. Can we talk?

The Overhaul of Humanity is not a small thing. The words I've used to describe this phenomenon are dramatic because the event is dramatic.

It is going to involve (indeed, it is already involving) every aspect of our lives: our governance and politics, our economics and financial stability, our commerce and industry, our social conventions and constructions, our educational systems and approaches, our religions and beliefs, our customs and traditions—in fact, our entire Cultural Story.

We can participate in the Overhaul of Humanity or we can merely witness it—but we cannot stop it. *Nor would we want to.*

This can be the greatest thing that has happened to our species since our appearance on this planet. The years just ahead, and some of the trials and tribulations we're going to see, can bring our planet to a new and wonderful place when the process is complete. And the process *will* be complete in a relatively short period of time.

And you can help bring *about* that completion if you choose to.

You don't have to simply read this

Life is inviting you to not have this be a book that you simply read. Life is inviting you to have this be an *experience* in which you *participate*. This is your opportunity to *join* me and others from around the world in the conversation that is being initiated here. You may do so at any time by simply stopping your reading, marking your place, then getting on the Internet and navigating to…

www.TheGlobalConversation.com

There, click on the icon labeled *The Storm Before the Calm*. Find and post any comment you wish at the numbered "Conversation" you're currently reading. (You'll notice that this book is not broken down into "Chapters," but rather, into "Conversations.")

At this special website, there's also a separate icon inviting you to post your ideas, your thoughts, your concepts, and your inspirations regarding the contents of Humanity's New Cultural Story. It is for this purpose that you have come to this material.

> We can participate in the Overhaul of Humanity or we can merely witness it, but we cannot stop it.

If you are like many others, you have long been asking, "What can I do? How can I help make things better?" This is an answer to that question.

The New Cultural Story co-created here by adding your insights and inspirations and heartfelt hopes and dreams for our world will be placed before humanity in a separate book: *Our Collective Dream: A New Cultural Story for Humanity.* This will be a book read around the world, and a book that *you co-author.*

So what you are reading now is not an ordinary text. This is your gateway to participation in what I am clear could very well be The Conversation of the Century. Your voice is valuable and needed in this exchange, in order that the exchange itself may sparkle with the vitality of a wide variety of ideas, insights, and visions. So do, please, consider *interacting* with this book, as well as reading it, yes?

POINTS I HOPE YOU WILL REMEMBER...

- A major shift is occurring on our planet.

- There is nothing to be afraid of if we all play our role in this shift.

- Our role is easy to play, and can actually be fun.

- What Life is inviting us to change is our Old Cultural Story.

ACTION I HOPE YOU WILL TAKE...

- Check out the website that has been specially created to allow the conversation that has been started here to continue. Go to *www.TheGlobalConversation.com* and see what you think.

- Return to that website anytime during your reading of this book that you see something you want to discuss further. Create your own Topic Board if you don't find the subject you wish to discuss already being explored there.

THE ANSWERS TO 'WHY' AND 'WHEN'

As we contemplate all that's occurring on our planet these days, it is fair to ask, "Does this _have_ to happen? _Why_ is this happening?"

The answer is yes, it has to happen. What is happening is happening because Life Itself is happening—and all of life moves in cycles, according to a formula. This formula requires that life progress through phases, based on principles of functionality, adaptability, and sustainability.

Whenever the _functionality_ of life in any of its many forms is threatened, it _adapts_ that manifestation, thus rendering itself _sustainable_ in a _new_ form.

This is the reason for the human experience that we call _death_. Death is not the end of life at all, but the continuation of life through the adaptation of the manifestation of a given life form, thus rendering that life sustainable in a new form.

This is true of _everything in existence_. Nothing "dies," and you cannot "kill" a thing. Not anything at all. You cannot kill a person, you cannot kill an animal, you cannot kill a plant.

This is important to understand during this time, especially, for there are those who have died, and those who will die, during this Overhaul of Humanity, and it is both helpful and healing to know that death is not a process that _takes_ a life, it is a process that _changes_ a life.

We miss their presence here with us—we miss them terribly—but we need not mourn for them. The new form they have embraced has brought them great joy.

> Wouldn't this mean that it's a splendid idea for us to end our own lives in our present form?

I get that question a lot, from people in many audiences and many cultures. My answer is always no. The soul's departure from this physical life is never a sadness, but always a joy, whenever and however it happens.

This does not mean, though, that it is a "good idea" to simply exit this physical life. The soul's agenda is what is being served here on the earth, and if the soul's agenda is complete, the right and perfect circumstances will be co-created for its departure. But those circumstances will never be artificially produced by the mind.

Just as it is a joy to leave the physical body, so is it a joy to stay, and if life in the physical is not a joy, it is because we are not looking at it from the perspective of the soul, but rather, trying to figure it out with our mind.

Life will never make sense to the mind. It will only make sense; and can only produce long-term, sustained happiness, peace, and joy when embraced from the perspective of the soul.

The trick then, if we are not happy in life, is not to leave the body, but to join the soul. This can be done while one is with the body. Yet most people are not bringing the soul into their daily experience.

Before this conversation is over, I will share with you exactly how to do that. And when you communicate with your soul you will understand fully what is going on here—on our planet, I mean. You will know that when the ability of *any* life form to continue in its present expression is compromised, that life form adapts its expression to allow it to immediately become sustainable again. It is in this way that life renders itself eternal.

Now there's no questioning that the life expression that we call Earth (what some have come to name Gaia) has had its ability to continue in its present expression compromised. The conditions leading to this threatening circumstance have been created in part by the human life forms inhabiting the Earth. Those human forms, in turn, have had their own expression threatened.

In short, neither the planet nor its people can continue to go on as they have been.

Don't worry. They won't.

Having reached the limit of its ability to produce sustainability in the earth's environment under present conditions, the Cycle of Life is now playing its effect, *adapting* all life forms in this environment, so that all life expression here may once again be rendered sustainable.

In other words, life on Earth is changing in order to continue. The fact that it is changing is the *guarantee* that it will continue.

So that's the *why* of what's going on. Before I get to the *when*, let me explain where that question that was asked just above came from.

Voices that differ

A conversation is not a "conversation" if it's a monologue. So from the very moment that I contemplated having this conversation with you through this book, I knew I wanted to avoid creating a single-voice oration, a soliloquy, a sermon or homily.

It's all very nice to invite you to jump into a discussion online, but that doesn't change what's appearing here—which *would*, in fact, be a monologue.

> Neither the planet nor its people can continue to go on as they have been.

Unless it wouldn't. Unless I could find a way to convert what could come off as a "lecture" into an actual conversation, right on these pages.

Here's what I came up with: I could create a "dialogue" growing out of conversations *that have already taken place.*

I could include here the thoughts, questions, and comments of other people, not just my own—offered in *their voice.* I could have a "conversation" that has been *retrieved* from my *memories* of previous exchanges with others.

In this way I could give voice to some who differ with what's on these pages. I think that's important. Voices that differ are voices that enlarge the scope of every conversation. They are also voices that represent a great many people. I hope we hear voices that differ in the online dialogue as well.

As for the voices that differ here, in this book…let me explain where they could come from.

I've been sharing the ideas being explored here for a good while, on the road. During a long string of evening lectures and weekend workshops, television appearances and talk show guestings, I've received some pretty tough questions and engaged in many vivid, spritely, sometimes challenging and once-in-a-while mildly aggressive exchanges—all of which have been totally okay with me, because I knew that all of them were serving me.

They were showing me where my thinking was perhaps a bit fuzzy, when my logic was perhaps faulty, which of my comments were hitting the nail on the head, and, in general, how other people were thinking about these same issues.

Over my 20 years as a member of the working press, I trained my mind to remember such encounters, often word for word—especially the more memorable ones—and I knew that I could bring the essence of these exchanges forward with the slightest stimulation.

So I thought, if anything I put down as I wrote this book brought back memories of one of those prior conversations, I could include my memory of it here. In that way, the present expression would not be just a monologue, with me rambling on and on from my point of view, but a "monoconvologue"—a monologue that includes conversations derived from previous dialogues.

Conversations not simply quoted, but inserted into the narrative flow *as if they were happening now.* I could dialogue with a *composite voice* of the many folks who have dialogued with me in the past.

A conversation with humanity

The more I thought about it, the more I liked the idea. So I decided to do it! And *that's* where the question that just popped into the narrative above came from. You'll be hearing from this "composite voice" on the pages that follow as well.

And what kinds of people comprise this composite voice? Who will be represented in these remembered exchanges?

Well, my prior explorations of the life-changing ideas presented here have taken place with folks all over the world, from Denmark to Norway to Sweden to France, from South Korea to South America, from Ireland to Poland, from Jamaica to Japan…from the steps of Machu Picchu to the steps of the Great Wall of China, from Red Square in Moscow to Vatican Square in Rome, from down under (Australia and New Zealand) to up over (Iceland), from Central West Africa to Central America, from across the United Kingdom to across the United States.

The inquiries and the opinions I've heard in these many places and from these many sources reflect a wide range of cultures, backgrounds, religious affiliations, political convictions, and social conventions, making for a spirited—and definitely not one-sided—*monoconvologue.*

And when *you* add *your* point of view later, in the online discussion, we will really have what I believe our species could truly benefit from right now: a *conversation with humanity.*

So, on the pages that follow, you'll get a glimpse of what people from all over the world have been thinking and asking about our tumultuous times and about the messages that I'm sharing, which I believe could change our world. I'll present their views here in a dialogue format, so that you can experience the exchanges very much as they originally took place, yes?

Now then, back to where I was going…

The *when* of the Overhaul

Several famous prognostications appear to indicate that the time of our species' next great evolutionary step is now.

Looking back, we have seen that Life Cycles are actually not that difficult to predict. Beginning in ancient times, people began to observe certain rhythms in events. Wise ones listened carefully to oral histories and began keeping track of the cycles. They used their observations to estimate the timing of *future* cycles.

This estimate of timing is what we find in the prognostications of Nostradamus, the prophecies of religious figures from all of the world's great religions, the predictions of the Maya Calendar, etc., many of which point to *this very moment* in human history as being significant.

Wikipedia tells us "that numerous cases of prophecy exist among the Native American populations," and that "the Onondaga and Hopi, among others, have prophecies that appear to relate to the times we are entering now.

"For example, the Onondaga talk of a time when the water will not be fit to drink from the streams. This, they say, will signify the beginning of a period they call *the great purification*, where the peoples will go through immense trials to purify themselves of the corrupting influences that have beset them.

"This, they say, will be seen as a period of joy for those who understand what is happening and engage this period as a time of purification, but will be a period of immense suffering for those who cling to their... worldview and lifestyles."

There was a big twinkle in my eye and a huge smile on my face as I read this prophecy, because I couldn't have put it better myself. That is exactly what I have come here to tell *you*. We are in for a period of *joy*— yet this period will include suffering for sure if we insist on clinging to our old worldview and lifestyles.

Just look at what that old worldview produced in *just the few months before this book was published...*

- Several nations had their future altered forever by revolutions.

- Other countries were devastated by the worst natural disasters in decades.

- People around the world saw their individual lives continue to be dismantled by a global financial meltdown that began 24-months earlier.

Add all that has happened in our world *since* then and we may well understand why much of humanity is looking to its future a bit nervously, wondering...Is this just the beginning of what the final month of that much-talked-about year, 2012, will bring? What lies ahead, not just in December 2012, but beyond?

POINTS I HOPE YOU WILL REMEMBER...

- The Overhaul of Humanity is part of a natural process by which life sustains itself.

- What would be beneficial right now is a conversation with humanity.

- The scope and sweep of events tells us that the Overhaul of Humanity has already begun; the time is now.

ACTION I HOPE YOU WILL TAKE...

- Think about ways in which you may be clinging to an old worldview and lifestyle. What does this mean to you? How does this look?

- Contemplate what's been going on in this world and in your life between the time this book was written (early summer, 2011) and now. Ask yourself, does it feel as if a "shift" is taking place? Perhaps begin a personal journal about all that you're observing, as part of your process.

- Begin thinking about what *you* would put into a New Cultural Story for humanity if you were asked to write it. (Which you *are* being asked to do, right here.)

THE ONE THING
WE KNOW FOR SURE

THE MAJOR DISRUPTIONS IN life as we know it will not be ending soon. Not before and not immediately after December 2012.

Yet—and I say this again, because it is important—things are not what they seem.

What is happening is not The End of History, but The Beginning of a New Era; not The Death of Modern Society, but The Birthing of a New Civilization.

Therefore, living in fear and apprehension, nervous caution and skittish timidity, warily searching for a safe place, hoarding food and hunkering down, preparing for a caveman survival mentality to overcome every human being on the earth as all the structures, conveniences, and technologies of our world simultaneously collapse, is not the answer.

The answer is to get *into* the game, not get *out of* the game by running from the playing field. And the game is not The Survival Game, the game is The Creation Game.

The answer is to join in the co-creation of magnificent days to come. I have something specific to suggest that we can all do, and it's so easy we'll wonder what took us so long to just jump in and do it.

My suggestion is that we all engage in a conversation with humanity—the part of humanity that we can personally touch.

That's it? Have a conversation? That's the Big Solution to Everything?

That's it. And yes, that *can* be the Big Solution to Everything. Not directly, of course. But indirectly.

Doesn't seem like much of a solution to me.

It *can* be, I promise you. And I'll talk a bit more about the power of all this later. Right now let me just say that you can start your end of this "conversation with humanity" by simply telling everyone you know that if we *do not* play our part, some of those things *could* happen.

And so today, just as many years ago, it is exactly as American President Franklin Roosevelt said: *We have nothing to fear but fear itself.*

What it's all about—and what it's not

How to proceed *without* fear will become clearer to all of us when we realize that what is taking place now all over our planet *is* not what it seems.

It has nothing to do at its basis with politics, so the upheavals in governance are misplaced and will do little or nothing to change things.

It has nothing to do at its basis with economics, so the protests about economic disparities are misdirected and will do little or nothing to change things.

It has nothing to do at its basis with military might, so the use of military power to quell dissent or resolve an issue will do little or nothing to change things.

It may look as if it has to do with all of those things, and it has to do with none of those things. Yet if we do not know what it *does* have to do with, and if we're unwilling to look at what it *might* have to do with, we're lost. If we don't know what the problem *is*, how can we get the problem *solved*?

> What is needed here is not a revolution on the ground, it is a revolution in the mind.

The irony here is that we *want* to solve it! Not a single person I know wants this to go on forever. (It's true that there are some folks out there who are actually *welcoming* these events—joyously proclaiming that these occurrences herald the coming of Armageddon, the last battle between good and evil before the Day of Judgment, when they imagine that only they will be "saved" — but most human beings are yearning to see better times, not the end times.)

Indeed, what I observe everywhere I go is that the human race is losing patience with itself. We don't *want* the kind of world we've created. Like a dissatisfied artist standing back from the canvas, we've decided that we're not pleased with the picture we've painted.

We've also become very clear (finally) that we can't paint a *better* picture by using the same brush strokes in the same places with the same colors we used before.

Something's got to change.

It's time to tear up the canvas and start over.

It is this awareness that is producing the Overhaul of Humanity.

The solution to the problem

Let's go to the dictionary and look up that word.

OVERHAUL: a comprehensive examination and repair of something.

Ah, yes…the *repair* of something. Not the *destruction* of something, the *repair of something.* That's what this time on our planet is all about. A lot of people are running around declaring that this is the end of everything. It's not. It's the beginning. This is about repair, not destruction, of our world and our way of life.

In order for those repairs to be made, we have to be clear about what is needed.

What is needed here is not a revolution on the ground, it is a revolution in the mind.

It is our *thinking* we must change. In the past we kept trying to change conditions on the ground, and even when we did manage to do so (every so often we found a Band-aid that helped), the same old (*age-old*) problems eventually reemerged—because nothing had been altered in our *mindset.*

All of that is changing. Large numbers of people are "getting" this now. And so, we are going to weather this storm, you and I. We're going to give our children, and theirs, a wonderful world in which to live. We're about to turn a page in human history.

Will you turn that page with me now?

POINTS I HOPE YOU WILL REMEMBER...

- We are approaching not the End of History, but the beginning of a New Era.

- It's time to tear up the canvas and start over.

- Large numbers of people are getting this, and we are going to weather this storm.

ACTION I HOPE YOU WILL TAKE...

- Start the conversation with humanity by telling everyone you know about what you're reading here.

THE FIRST BELIEF
WE HAVE TO CHANGE

As WE MOVE INTO A new era, the first thing we have to do is take responsibility for our past.

Now, now, don't run from that. This is not about taking *blame*, it's about taking *control*.

I'm not talking about "beating ourselves up" for what's gone wrong or what's gone before. What I *am* talking about is a moving into gentle, quiet knowing, a soft and compassionate holding, of a simple truth: We are not the victims here.

What's happening in our lives and all over our planet right now is good, but that goodness will be wasted if we do not see what is so; if we insist on imagining that we are somehow the victims of what is occurring; if we declare with fist-pounding certainty that these things are happening *to* us, not *through* us.

And so…

The first belief we're going to have to change is the belief in our own "bystanderness."

That manufactured word captures perfectly the thought held by many that we are helpless, hapless, and hopeless, forced to suffer silently and shiver fearfully in the face of what's going on and what appears to be coming. This is a false thought, an inaccurate thought, a misleading thought. More important, it's a dysfunctional thought. It causes us, quite literally, to *dysfunction*.

So let's get rid of this thought. Having turned the page, let's now turn our attention to an important awareness. Let this fourth conversation that we are having here, then, be about cause.

Acknowledging our role in the scheme of things

All of us can easily see, simply by looking around us, just how bad things have gotten on this planet. But now, a question…

Why

isn't

anybody

asking

why

?

This is not one of the Seven Simple Questions that I mentioned earlier. This is a question that stands all by itself, alone. It *precedes* the Seven Simple Questions, and creates a context for them.

Not enough people are asking this preceding question, much less answering it. I'm going to do both. It's part of that first belief we have to change. I'm going to stop being a bystander.

In a little booklet I wrote in Spring, 2011, I said something that I believe is worth sharing again here: Events on the earth are not created by Unseen Forces. We're not here subject to the whims of the gods, or, as William Shakespeare put it, suffering "the slings and arrows of outrageous fortune."

Even in the case of geophysical events, we are not entirely at the mercy of the elements. It may seem as though we are, but we're not.

Take earthquakes, for instance. They are real, they are occurring, and they are *something that we are at some level creating.*

Take hurricanes and tornadoes and typhoons and tidal waves and tsunamis. They are all occurring, and they are all *something that we are at some level creating.*

Take global warming, for instance. It is real, it is occurring, and it is *something that we are at some level creating.*

Or, for that matter, take the incredible and rapid spread of bacterial diseases sweeping across the earth. This, too, is *something that we are at some level creating.*

Of course, we don't have any intention of admitting any of this. At least, not the members of humanity's "establishment."

In a horrifying example of non-leadership, the U.S. House of Representatives voted 240-184 in the spring of 2011 to *defeat* a resolution that simply said that "climate change is occurring, is caused largely by human activities, and poses significant risks for public health and welfare."

Imagine that.

Now...are "we, the people" creating these events *consciously?* Of course not. Yet could we be creating these events *unconsciously?* Absolutely. Through our unconscious (that is to say, our unthinking or short-sighted) behaviors.

> You're asking me to accept a lot here. No one that I know sits around deciding to produce an earthquake—and they couldn't do it if they wanted to. And there's no proof that global warming is "caused largely by human activities."

Would you agree to this—that human beings are more than passive observers in the rollout of life?

> Depends on what you're talking about. If you're talking about tornadoes and stuff...

Well, let me ask you this. How many underground nuclear weapons tests do you think we can conduct before the massive explosions we produce loosen or dislodge the interconnecting plates that form the substructure of the planet's undergirdment, eventually resulting in earthquakes?

How much carbon can we emit before we overload the earth's natural greenhouse mechanism and cause significant warming of the planet, such that the rising temperatures of its massive waters produce geothermal conditions generating wind variations violent enough to call them hurricanes and tornadoes?

And please let me read a couple of paragraphs from the April 2011 issue of *Scientific American:*

"For more than 50 years microbiologists have warned against using antibiotics to fatten up farm animals. The practice, they argue, threatens human health by turning farms into breeding grounds of drug-resistant bacteria.

> Human beings are more than passive observers in the rollout of life.

"Farmers responded that restricting antibiotics in livestock would *devastate the industry* and significantly *raise costs* to consumers."

Would someone tell me how it could do both?

If it significantly raised prices (do you think meat-buyers would pay a bit more to live a lot longer?), how would the industry be devastated? The way the oil industry was devastated when gas prices shot up 30%?

This lapse in logic notwithstanding...who do you suppose won *that* debate? (Follow the money trail.)

Now the good news

Of course, I'm fully aware that there are those people who roundly poo-poo the notion that human activity has anything whatsoever to do with any of this, but I am here to declare (along with the overwhelming majority of the world's scientists, geophysicists, and medical researchers) that these activities are, in fact, intertwined, that we live in an interconnected world where one thing definitely and invariably leads to another, and that humanity is no more immune from causality than any other element of life itself.

To put this simply, we are at least *part* of the problem.

That's good news. Because if we are part of the problem, we can also be part of the solution. If we are *not* part of the problem, then we have naught but to endure it. Yet if we *are* part of the problem (and can admit that we are), then we are not utterly at the mercy of Unseen Forces.

With regard to human affairs, as opposed to physical occurrences, this is obviously true. We are *completely* at cause in the matter of the geo-political upheavals of humanity.

> Well, yes and no. It's true that political disasters are not caused by nature, but they are the result of *human* nature, and that is equally uncontrollable.

Really? I mean, is this true? Are human beings "just the way they are," with certain proclivities so "built in" that there is nothing we can do about our more violent, competitive, or survival-oriented nature?

> Hasn't that pretty much been proven? Do you see human nature changing much?

Well, I think this is something we're about to decide. The collective called humanity, I mean.

We are about to decide—and to announce our decision through our thoughts, words, and actions—what we consider to be true about us, and about our *nature*.

We are also about to decide whether we are ready and willing to change what *has been* true about our nature, due to the immaturity of our species, in earlier years. It is this choice that will be tomorrow's declaration; it is this demonstration that will be our new manifesto.

> If we are part of the problem, we can also be part of the solution.

To me it seems perfectly clear: we can no longer move forward, advancing our own evolutionary process as a species, by demonstrating the behaviors of the past. It is as the late Walt Kelly's comic strip character *Pogo* memorably pronounced: "We have met the enemy, and he is us."

Yet if most people continue to insist that what has got to change is *unchangeable*—that the basic nature of our species is simply what it is, and that there is no altering it—then we are surely doomed.

There is nothing for us to do but cut and run, hoard and hide, surviving as best we can while the world falls apart around us.

On the other hand, if we *renounce* the Doctrine of Impossibility, if we *reject* the notion of our impotence, if we *abandon* the thought that we have no control over our behavior because of our very nature, a New Future opens to us; a New Tomorrow beckons. It can be the Future of Our Preference, the Tomorrow of Our Chosen Reality.

Victims or creators?

The first step in the manifestation of this grander eventuality is the embracing of a grander truth about the role we are playing, and *have* played.

We must decide: is life something that is happening *to* us or something that is happening *through* us?

Even with regard to geophysical conditions and events on our planet (over which, at first glance, we might imagine we have no control), we must decide that we do have a collaborative role to play in how those occur and affect us.

> Is life something that is happening *to* us or something that is happening *through* us?

The Japanese calamity of 2011 is a remarkable example. Even if we assert that we had no long-range role whatsoever in the earthquake and tsunami (a position that I, personally, am not prepared to take), there is not one of us who can deny that humanity *definitely* had a role in the nuclear disaster that followed—and can have a big role in avoiding these disasters in the future.

There are those who understand this perfectly…

On May 30, 2011, Germany formally announced plans to *abandon nuclear energy completely* within 11 years.

Eight of the nation's 17 plants that had been temporarily shut down would remain closed permanently, the government said. The remaining nine plants would be shut down by 2022.

This is a striking example of a world waking up. We're beginning to understand and to acknowledge the role that we, ourselves, have played in creating the storm before the calm. We're beginning to take a stand—not just to *under*stand, but to *take* stand.

POINTS I HOPE YOU WILL REMEMBER...

- We are not the victims here, we are at least part of the problem.

- We can no longer move forward with the behaviors of the past.

- We don't need to take blame, we need to take control.

ACTION I HOPE YOU WILL TAKE...

- Change any belief you may have that you are a "bystander" in the way life is proceeding on the earth.

- Renounce the Doctrine of Impossibility.

THE MOST DARING THING THAT HUMANITY COULD DO RIGHT NOW

I'M NOT SURE WHERE this item originally came from, but someone sent it to me in an email and it articulates cleverly and perfectly what I'm saying here:

> An important job had to be done and Everybody was sure that Somebody would do it. Anybody could have done it, but Nobody did it. Somebody got angry about that because it was Everybody's job. Everybody thought that Anybody could do it, but Nobody realized that Everybody wouldn't do it. It ended up that Everybody blamed Somebody when Nobody did what Anybody could have done.

I've come here to invite you to decide right now not to do "nothing." Choose to do "something."

I hope I am not being too redundant when I say that life will not be the same when the Overhaul of Humanity is complete, yet if we all do "something," the changes will be for the better.

Some souls will have left our planet, that is true (and we deeply honor them for their sacrifice of this present life on behalf of us all), but most souls are going to stay on the earth in order to move evolution in this particular environment forward, and to assist in dealing with the aftermath of events—doing so in such a way that the changes *will* be for the better.

I don't personally believe there is much question about whether you and I will do "something" rather than "nothing." You are ready, and so am I, to take up our positions, to hold up our end, to do our part. And we are in the majority. *All we need is to be given something to do.* A lot of people just don't know *what* they can do, and so they assume there's *nothing* they can do. That's just not true.

> Most of us
> are embracing
> doctrines that are
> simply not true.

There's plenty to talk about, and that's all we really have to do. So it can be easy and fun. And here's more good news: You won't be alone.

We are here. All of us who are involved in this conversation. And in just a bit I'll place on the table one possible way that we might *leverage* the fact that we are all here together.

Then we can all ask together, "Why?" Why are the conditions on our planet today the way they are? People are not asking why either because they have asked the question many times before to no benefit, or, worse yet, because they think they already have the answer.

Some of them think that the answer has to do with the political doctrine of other people. If only people would embrace *their* political doctrine, everything would work out.

Some of them think that the answer has to do with the religious doctrine of other people. If only people would embrace *their* religious doctrine, everything would work out.

Some of them think that the answer has to do with the economic doctrine of other people. If only people would embrace *their* economic doctrine, everything would work out.

All of them are wrong.

The reason our species remains unable to create for *all* of us on the earth the life that we say we *want* for all of us on the earth is that most of us are embracing doctrines that are simply not true.

This is what we need to stop doing. It is our cultural story that has to change.

> You've used the phrase "cultural story" now a number
> of times. Help me understand exactly what you're referring
> to. You're talking about our religions, right?

Oh, much more than that.

A Cultural Story is a very large tale that we tell our children, and that they tell theirs, of "how it is," of "who we are," of "the way things work," and of the purpose of it all.

It's the story that was told to *us*—and that was told to those who *told* it to us. It's the narration that we heard every day of our lives, in one form or another.

It is the Passed-Down Understanding.

It is the Inherited Hypothesis.

It is the Standard Supposition.

It is the Memory Myth.

It is a story that provides the *foundation* for our religions—as well as our political process, our economic system, and all of our social interaction. It influences our lives at every level: our courting and relationship rituals, our sexual mores, our mating and marriage models, our parenting approaches, our conditions of friendship...*everything.*

Precisely because this story is so pervasive, this is what we should be talking about. Yet it is what so many people will *not* talk about.

> Why?

I think it's because folks know that this *is* the real problem. *Their story is the problem.* Yet it is a story that is *sacred* to them, an oft-told tale to which they fiercely adhere and which they do not intend to relinquish or abandon. To do so would seem to them to be abandoning their ancestors, devaluing their traditions, dishonoring their history.

A wonderful minister whose church I attended nearly 20 years ago, Rev. Terry Cole-Whittaker, used to ask in her Sunday morning sermons, "Who would you have to make 'wrong' in order for you to be 'right'?"

She hit the bull's eye with that question.

People know that if they change their story—their group story or even their individual story—they will have changed their minds about virtually everything of any importance that any *person* of any importance in their life has ever said.

And they know that this will affect their sense of *who they are,* their idea of *what is so,* even their plans and strategies for *where they are going.*

Such massive change is very difficult for people. For many people. Perhaps for most people. Most would rather keep things as they are, even if things are not so good, than make a change, because change produces the *unknown*—and that which people do not know, they often fear.

It is *fear* that stops most folks from changing. They may not like things the way they are, but at least they know what that *is*. And so, conversations that clearly could lead to significant *change* have not been enthusiastically welcomed or well tolerated.

> It is *fear* that stops most folks from changing.

And to give a full answer, I think it's about more than just fear of the unknown. I think that many people know that if they really sat down together and objectively examined what they are repeating by rote to their children, they would see the folly in it. In a lot of it they would see just how wrong they are, how off base they've been, how misguided and mistaken and how incomplete their awareness is.

Thus, humanity appears to be stuck...*one conversation from paradise.*

We'll have to do what we've never done before

Imagine, a single conversation that could change everything. Many people—perhaps most people—might never have that conversation... unless they were gently encouraged to get into it. That's where you come in.

> But what could one conversation possibly reveal or involve that could bring us to paradise?

Well, it would be one conversation, but with many people. I'm saying that if hundreds of people...let's say thousands, many thousands... found themselves in the same conversation in their small social groups or church gatherings or family parties, whatever...or if many folks were suddenly talking about the same thing on social networking Internet sites, as an example…this single conversation, with many people in many times and places, could result in us ultimately—and relatively quickly, actually—creating paradise on Earth.

The seed of this idea was planted when I was sitting around sharing a quiet conversation with a handful of people who'd come to Ashland, Oregon, to spend five days with my wife and me at our house for an event that we call The Homecoming.

(Each year a different small group—six to ten people or so—gathers with us for five days, exploring life on a very personal level.)

It was during the August 2010 Homecoming that someone remarked about the sheer power of some questions I'd been posing during our discussions. I called them the Seven Simple Questions.

"The whole world should be invited to ask and answer these questions!" someone exclaimed.

"Yes," I agreed, "it sometimes seems to me that if we all just ran around asking these seven simple questions, we'd be just one generation from paradise."

The ring of that phrase hit all of us at once. After a stunned silence in the room, someone in the group, a man from Great Britain, said, "Neale, that's something that should be said everywhere. You could start a global *movement* around that."

And so we did. Those of us in that room did, right then and there. And when some of us came back together for a planning session a few months later, we decided that we were not one *generation* from paradise…we could easily be just one *conversation* from paradise.

We simply needed to encourage everyone to have a simple conversation with as many others as they could, asking those Seven Simple Questions.

Out of that idea we created what we called The Conversations Movement. That man from the U.K., a chap named Steve Minchin, became its volunteer worldwide coordinator. And *that*, my friends, is how things happen. That's how things that change the world begin.

I have to admit, though, that as good as the whole idea was feeling, I found myself asking what you just asked right now…What could

> Will asking seven questions be enough?

possibly be said in one conversation that would create such an impact that it could begin humanity's march to Paradise? I mean, *will asking seven questions be enough?*

Upon deep reflection, here's what I realized:

Yes. Because those *particular* questions stimulate explorations of new ideas about who we are, about the real purpose of life, about who and what God is, and about our true relationship with each other. And because the purpose of such a conversation would not be to marginalize, ridicule, or abandon old beliefs, but simply to invite the consideration of new ones.

Yet to extend, and to *accept*, such an invitation will take courage. Human beings have been willing to consider new ideas—even so-called heretical ideas—in virtually every important area of human endeavor... except *the most critical area of all*: our most important personal and collective beliefs.

In order to consider new beliefs, we would have to do what we have routinely done in science, in medicine, and in technology, but have not had the courage to do in religion or in many matters of personal belief. We would have to be willing to *question the prior assumption.*

This would be the single most daring thing that humanity could do right now.

A formula that works

Change does not come easy in any field. As Max Planck, one of the fathers of quantum physics, once observed:

"A new scientific truth does not triumph by convincing its opponents and making them see the light, but rather because its opponents eventually die, and a new generation grows up that is familiar with it."

Or, as more whimsically paraphrased, "Science advances one funeral at a time."

(Source: *Wikiquotes*—http://en.wikiquote.org/wiki/Max_Planck).

Still, at least Science *eventually* questions the basis on which a scientific conclusion was reached and, using this device, it one day comes up with even more answers, more brilliant solutions, more magnificent and miraculous outcomes.

Likewise, when Medicine comes up with an answer, those who engage in Medicine in any serious way eventually question the basis on which that conclusion was reached. And using this device, they come up with even more answers, more brilliant solutions, more magnificent and miraculous outcomes.

And so, too, is it in Technology.

This is a formula that works.

Yet with regard to the answers that we derive from Religion and from our other Cultural Beliefs, it doesn't matter how many funerals there have been. It doesn't matter how many generations have passed. Most people simply *refuse to question the prior assumption.* In fact, many have been known to declare that to do so is as act of *apostasy.*

This is the great tragedy of humanity. This is the greatest stumbling block of our species.

We have made breathtaking, almost unbelievable, advances in technology, medicine, and science precisely because those who practice these disciplines have ultimately avoided this stumbling block, even if it did take time.

> It is possible that all we think we know could be wrong.

Over decades and centuries they have been willing to make one key statement that most people who are officially associated with religious or cultural beliefs dare not make:

It is possible that all we think we know could be wrong.

At the very least it could be incomplete.

If humanity would engage in a global conversation about our religions, our beliefs, and our Cultural Story that began with this key statement, that conversation could result in new ideas that could produce new solutions that would make the advances we have seen in medicine, science, and technology look like child's play.

We would create the life for which we have dreamed, the outcomes for which we were destined, the human experience *for which we were designed.*

Many people are actually producing this outcome for themselves individually right now, in the present moment. If they all simply started *talking about it,* they could spread this outcome to our entire species within one generation—one conversation at a time.

So yes, I think it would be wonderful for all of us to talk.

Let me put it more urgently. I think we *need* to talk.

Not quarrel, not argue, not fight, not contradict or debate or dispute or wrangle, just converse—speaking with a gentle passion, listening with an open mind, sharing with a tolerant and tender heart, exploring with a generous spirit, and concluding with a willing invitation to not let the conversation end, but to talk and to share again, as part of an ongoing exchange that need never end.

Humanity *can* create, if it so chooses, a *new* Cultural Story—a fresh set of beliefs about who we are and why we are here and what is really "so" about each other and about life...and yes, even a new—or, to put it a better way, an *enlarged*—set of beliefs about God, so that Divinity *may finally be rendered functional,* and not merely *doctrinal.*

The role you were destined to play

We took a look earlier at the role that human beings have played in bringing about our present circumstance. I also spoke of the role we can play right now in bringing about a change in those circumstances more quickly. Now I want to say something daring about that.

It is a role I believe you have come here to play.

You have come here—to physical form, to this place called Earth, at this particular and critical time in history—*to participate in the evolution of our species.*

I realize that this may sound grandiose, yet I believe deeply that it's true. This is not the only reason you are here, of course. You are here for reasons having to do with your own evolution, your own experience. Yet the more of the latter you achieve, the more of the former you desire, for you realize ultimately that they are one and the same.

But let's talk about it. Let's see what's in *your* head about this.

Do you believe that you arrived here at this time *by accident?* Do you think that the events occurring all around you are somehow *out of sequence?* Do you imagine that things are happening *that should not be happening?*

Do you hold the idea that the timing of your life upon the earth during these crucial passages is a coincidence? Is it your thought that the impeccable synchronization of your arrival with the arrival of This Moment is *by chance?*

Let me know. Engage in this conversation. We're talking about it now at *www.TheGlobalConversation.com.*

Here is my own thought about it: No. That is not how life works. In life, nothing happens by chance. Life proceeds out of your intentions for it. *Even your intentions before birth.* You have a soul. You are much more than simply a body with a mind. And "life" for you extends far beyond the limits of your present physical incarnation.

If you do not believe this, you may find it difficult to easily or comfortably embrace the idea that part of your journey on Earth is to assist in the evolution of your species.

Such an agenda will feel huge, out of reach, beyond your ability. But it is not. You are very able to offer the gentle assistance life invites you to provide right now. And if you're willing to offer it, you could truly—I am going to say it again—help to change the world.

POINTS I HOPE YOU WILL REMEMBER...

- If we all agree not to "do nothing" during the Overhaul of Humanity, coming changes will be for the better.

- Most people are embracing doctrines that are simply not true.

- Because our cultural story, which contains those doctrines, is so pervasive, we need to be talking about it.

- We could be just one conversation from paradise— if enough of us had that conversation, and ignited it, with others.

- You are destined to play a role in the evolution of our species.

ACTION I HOPE YOU WILL TAKE...

- Decide to learn all that you can about our Old Cultural Story and what it's been telling us, so that you can discuss it with others.

- Contribute to the writing of proposals for our New Cultural Story by going to the website at *www.TheGlobalConversation.com.*

- Begin conversations wherever you go in a gentle, congenial way about both the old story and the new—and especially about the Seven Simple Questions, which we will discuss here soon.

THIS IS ABOUT
YOUR EVOLUTION, TOO

THE GOOD NEWS IS that to affect the course of human history you don't have to be a public speaker or a best-selling writer or a television presenter or a group facilitator or a workshop giver or whatever else you might think you have to be to make a difference. You don't have to have a public profile or reach spiritual mastery or commit huge amounts of time or pledge tons of money.

And…should you choose to *accept the call,* you'll be working not just on behalf of humanity at large, but on your own behalf as well.

So here's the scoop:

Your participation in the evolution of our species is achieved *through the work you do with your own soul.*

I meant it when I said that humanity could be just one conversation from paradise. That conversation begins with a talk that you have with *yourself.* It involves you *questioning the prior assumption*—every assumption you may have had about yourself, about your world, and about life itself.

It could then involve you having a similar conversation with others. This is what The Conversations Movement is all about.

> I love this idea of working with my own soul to personally evolve…but how does talking about all this with others accomplish that?

The work of your soul is not limited to the self. The work of the soul is to also *care for the souls of others*. It is to care for all souls. For your soul realizes that there is really Only One Soul, individualized in countless forms. Thus, caring for all souls is caring for Ourselves; working with all souls is working with one's own soul.

That is why the impulse to help each other is built into our genes; it is coded within our species. We care for each other, and we do what we can to show it. We have a "soul contract" to do so. I'm convinced of it. We all, each of us, *feel* this impulse.

> Your participation in the evolution of our species is achieved *through the work you do with your own soul.*

One way, one very easy way, that we can show that we care for each other is to enter with others into the same vivid and vital conversation we enter into with ourselves. In other words, do our soul searching together. Because the process of soul searching can be a lonely experience. Yet it need not be.

When a person enters into soul searching, that person can change. And when a group enters into soul searching together, that *group* can change. And when a whole society enters into soul searching together, that entire *society* can change. Soon the collective culture of *many* societies changes. Then, the World Entire.

It all starts with you deeply questioning yourself. And then carrying the questions to others.

The choice is yours

And so that is what I am describing here when I refer to "the work you do with your own soul." It is one form of soul work. It is obviously not the only form, but it can be a powerful form. It is a form so powerful that it can transform a person, a group, a society, a culture, and a world.

You're not "required" to do any of this work, of course. Nor are you required to do it in a particular way. You can do this work with your individual soul, or you can do it with your individual soul *and* with the collective souls of others. The choice is yours.

How do you work with your soul? How can I even
connect with my soul to do this "soul searching"?

Fair questions. No one teaches this stuff in high school. Very little is
written about it. Churches don't even get very deeply into it. But we are
going to here. I will share with you in this conversation all that I know
about how to connect with your soul, *daily*, in a wonderful way that
brings you right into the soul's experience and allows you to access the
soul's wisdom. So stick around for that. It's a three-step process that has
changed people's lives.

Can I ask you what may seem like an insolent question?

Of course. Ask me anything.

What is the basis of all of this for you? You keep talking
about seven simple questions. Who made 'em up? Where
did they come from? What makes them so magical for
you? For that matter, where is *all* this stuff about an "overhaul" and the need for a "new cultural story" coming from?

The basis of all that's here

That isn't insolent at all. I should think you'd want to know that. So
thanks for letting me explain.

Just over a decade and a half ago I had an experience in which I was
inspired by The Divine. I wrote a book about it, called *Conversations with God*.

That book created a global spiritual publishing phenomenon, selling
over a million copies, being translated into 35 languages, and remaining
on the *New York Times* bestseller list for 137 weeks.

During the time since then, eight other books in this ongoing dialogue have been released, six of those also making the *Times* bestseller list.

I am not telling you this to boast. I am telling you this to create a
context within which to consider what I've been saying here—and all
that I am going to say next.

God has brought a life-changing message to our world and, given the combined sales of all the *CWG* books and the hand-to-hand sharing of them, millions of people have been touched by it. There is a reason for this. It did not happen by chance.

The Overhaul of Humanity (remember that definition—OVERHAUL: a comprehensive examination and repair of something) is under way, and I believe that the sudden appearance of the *CWG* material is all a part of that.

Does this mean that I am somehow a messiah? No. It means that we all are. For the most important, the most prominent, and the most repeated message of *Conversations with God* is that all of us are having conversations with God all the time. We're simply calling them something else.

We're calling them moments of "inspiration." Or "women's intuition." Or a "psychic hit." Or a "bright idea." Or a "deep insight." Or an "epiphany." We call the results of such encounters "serendipity" or "coincidence" or "chance."

We deny, deny, *deny* that they could actually be interactions with the Divine because we've been culturalized to hold ourselves as being *unworthy of such experiences*. Indeed, to claim to have had personal contact directly from God is considered by many to be blasphemy.

> It is time for *Conversations with Humanity.*

Yet throughout human history women and men have experienced moments of deep connection with the heart and the source and the essence of life, by whatever name we call it, and across the span of time ordinary people have had extraordinary awakenings leading to both percipience and prescience.

Now it is time for all of us to claim that, and for a new conversation to take place. A conversation that proceeds from our conversations with God. Now it is time for us to have the conversation with ourselves that I just spoke of. And then, for all of us to have conversations with each other.

It is time for *Conversations with Humanity.*

For everywhere we turn today people are looking for wisdom, searching for clarity, seeking solutions, trying to figure out *just what went wrong with us* that we would now be acting the way we are acting—killing and maiming each other, ignoring the desperate needs of our fellow humans in spite of our basic impulse to care for each other, ruining our planet in spite of the fact that we say we love it, reaching, reaching, reaching endlessly for Bigger, Better, More while hundreds of thousands revolt because they have *never* had what others have right now.

The conversations I'm proposing can provide an avenue to wisdom, a roadway to clarity, a path to solutions for many. But they must be real dialogues, not simply the pontifications of those who think they have something important to say. They must be openings to mutual understanding, then mutual creation.

POINTS I HOPE YOU WILL REMEMBER...

- Your participation in the evolution of our species has to do with the work you do with your own soul.

- That work is about deep inquiry, or what we call "soul searching."

- The work of the soul is not limited to the self, but can involve the lifting of all other souls to peace and clarity.

- You are not required to do any of this work.

ACTION I HOPE YOU WILL TAKE...

- Read *Conversations with God—Book One* if you have not already done so or, if it has been some time since you read it, reread it now.

- Engage in the process of deep inquiry with your soul, using the Seven Simple Questions, which are outlined in the next conversation in this book.

- Continue the process of igniting conversations with others, centered around their own look at these questions.

QUESTIONS THAT VERY FEW
PEOPLE ARE WILLING TO ANSWER

OKAY, THE DARING STUFF starts now. I offer here a series of inquiries that it is going to take courage to engage.

It will take courage because the only answers people can offer are unsettling—no matter what those answers might be. The questions themselves are just simply upsetting.

(Unless they're not. They're upsetting to folks who don't want things changed, or even challenged. They're not to those who are now ready to say, "Enough. Enough already with the way things are. There's got to be another way.")

Okay…I assume you're "all in" because you're still here.

Nice.

I mean, really. Nice going.

The Greatest Revolution

We're talking here about questions and answers that could spark the biggest revolution ever to hit this planet. And that's saying a lot.

A search on *Wikipedia* under the word "revolutions" brings up a virtually endless catalogue of uprisings, beginning with the popular revolt in the Sumerian city of Lagash that deposed King Lugalanda and put the reformer Urukagina on the throne in 2380 B.C., ending with the revolutions that overturned governments in the Arab world in 2011.

Let me just give you part of this list, just to take a quick look at how people have been responding on this planet to how they've been governed....

We have seen literally hundreds of uprisings and revolutions across our history, including the Fall of the Roman Empire, the First of the Wars of Scottish Independence, the American Revolution, the French Revolution, the revolution in India, the Boer Revolt, revolutions all over South America, the European Revolutions of 1848; the revolutions in modern Hungary, in Yugoslavia, in Haiti, the dissolution of the Soviet Union by 1991...

...take my word for it. This is a *tiny* portion of a list that goes on and on and on...and ON. We've been "revolting" since the beginning of our gathering together in clans and tribes and then, nations.

What is this all about, do you think?

What do you imagine has been causing all of this? *Why do you think it never ends?* And what do you think could *make* it end?

I can tell you what it's about. And I can also tell you how to make it end, with One Final Revolution. Indeed, that's what *The Storm Before the Calm* is all about. What has been *causing* all of this for so long is that...

Human beings have been clear for a very long time that the way life has been constructed on this planet by those in power is *not the way it was intended to be lived.*

And so, since *forever*—for centuries and *millennia*—people on every spot on the globe have been agitating. They've wanted a new way of life—a new way of being human; a way that they know it was *intended* for them to be human.

Their agitations have continued right up to this present day. Even as this is being written, people in many places on Earth are still saying *No!* to the way things are, and are demanding change.

They're prepared to die for it. They *have* been dying for it. They're dying right now, as you're reading this.

But we are ready now, as a global community, for that dying to stop. We've had it. We're done. *There's got to be a better way.* We wonder, why don't those who seek to govern us *get it?* But they don't, so now we're seeing what I have been calling here the Overhaul of Humanity.

This is a revolution that will not ask people to die, but will simply ask people to inquire. It will invite people to make inquiries of themselves and others that could change everything in such a huge way that, *finally*, future violent revolutions may never again be necessary.

So let's look at these seven "dangerous" questions.

I like to place them into two groups. For me, they're easier to grapple with that way. So I've divided them into what I call the Three Persistent Questions and the Four Fundamental Questions of Life.

These are not *I gotcha* questions, designed to trap or trick anyone into anything. They are genuine inquiries, being asked (and you must ask them) sincerely, with purity of heart, not out of righteousness, not out of argumentativeness. And they are placed here gently, softly, for I recognize that most human beings, for all the reasons given earlier, are not comfortable discussing these things.

> The way life has been constructed on this planet by those in power is *not the way it was intended to be lived.*

The power structure on our planet is very happy about that, because real, honest-to-goodness exploration of these questions could lead to real honest-to-goodness examination of *what we're doing* right now on the planet—and *that* could just possibly result in a real honest-to-goodness *shift* in the *way* we are doing it...and in how we choose to be human.

Should *that* happen, as far as the power structure is concerned, The Game is Over. Life as we have been living *is* history, and this *will* be the end of it.

The Seven Simple Questions

The following inquiries, made in the depth of our own soul, and used by us to invite others into their own soul searching, could change the world.

THE THREE PERSISTENT QUESTIONS

1. How is it possible that 6.9 billion people can all claim to want the same thing (peace, security, opportunity, prosperity, happiness, and love) and be *singularly unable to get it?*

2. Is it possible that there is something we do not fully understand about life, *the understanding of which would change everything?*

3. Is it possible that there is something we do not fully understand about *ourselves*, about our *own* life and its purpose, *the understanding of which would shift our reality and alter our experience for the better, forever?*

These are powerful questions. They deserve answers. *They at least deserve being asked.* Yet are great numbers of people asking them? Are politicians? No. Presidents and prime ministers, kings and heads of state? No. Religious figures? No. Educators? Not many. Military generals and admirals? No. Leaders of business and industry? No. Ordinary people at their dinner table? Well, yes, possibly. Beginning now. Perhaps. Beginning now.

Ordinary people like you and I will now be asking these questions all over the planet. And when we finish asking the first three, we'll then move to...

THE FOUR FUNDAMENTAL QUESTIONS OF LIFE

1. Who am I?

2. Where am I?

3. Why am I where I am?

4. What do I intend to do about that?

I do not believe that one can ignore these questions and rapidly evolve. None of us can. We must end any personal confusion we may have around these questions (there are many other questions in life, but these are foundational), or we will go through our days and nights having no idea what we're doing or why we're doing it.

This is the situation with most people on the earth today. And that is the reason why the world is in the condition that it's in.

I did not move forward in my life until I answered the Four Fundamental Questions of Life. (And by the way, I answer them *daily*.

Sometimes *during* the day as events transpire. Used in this way, these questions are not only *in*formative, they are *trans*formative.)

And the first of these four is the real key. It unlocks everything. It invites us to look deeply at the biggest mystery, the mystery of our own identity. By that I don't mean, of course, our name. I mean *our identity in the cosmos.*

There is no "right answer" to this question, there is only the answer you give.

The second question seems simple, but its answer may not be.

Where am I?

Where do you conceive of yourself as being? That is, what is this place in which we experience our existence? How do you conceive of it? How do you hold it in your reality?

I am speaking here of how you hold it conceptually, yes? I'm not talking about your physical description of this place ("I live on planet Earth. It is the third rock from the sun...," etc.), I am referring to your conceptual understanding of this space. Is it a place of learning, a school?

Do you experience it as a place of testing, an examination room? Is it a place of proving or contesting or competing, like a giant racetrack or an athletic field, where some are winners and some are losers?

Do you *have* no conceptual reference point for this space, and truly conceive of it only as a physical location in a larger system of planets whizzing around a star?

What *is* this place in which we find ourselves? The mind begs to know... *Where am I?*

Again, there is no "right" answer to this question. Yet until I gave it *some* answer, I had no conceptual framework within which to hold my life's experience. And absent such a framework, those experiences themselves felt essentially meaningless. No different from those of a fly or an ant. I felt that I was simply a more sophisticated life form. I had a life expectancy and, barring unforeseen circumstances, I knew I would be here for *x* amount of time, but what *is* this place?

And then, the next question looms: *Why?*

Why *am* I where I am? Why am I not somewhere else? *Is* there a "somewhere else"? What is the *purpose* of my being in this time and place? *Is* there a purpose? Who would give it one?

I don't know how a person advances in their evolution without giving some thought—and eventually, some sort of answer—to these questions.

Many people respond to these questions with a curt "I don't know" and let it go at that. I couldn't do that. And I don't encourage any true students of life to do that. If they truly don't have an answer, I encourage them to create one. That is, *decide* what their answer is, out of pure intention. In this way they live their life from Intention rather than living their life by default.

A life lived by default is a life lived according to the Default Responses of the majority of people on the earth. I hope that none of you ever again chooses to live your life like that. Most of us have lived at least portions of our lives in this way, but we never have to again if we do not want to.

The last inquiry

This leads to the final question. Not just the final question in this series of seven, but what could be, metaphorically, The Final Important Question of Life: Having given your answers to all the other questions, you are invited to decide, *What do you intend to do about that?*

This is always the final question in life. In every situation, in every circumstance, in every moment that our experience presents, the question always and forever is: *What do I intend to do about that?*

Life proceeds out of your intentions for it. This is the fuel that drives the engine of creation in your life.

It is important to understand that life is nothing but energy. It is energy *organized*. And who does the organizing? *We do.* Surprisingly, the answer is…*us*. Life is pure energy that circles back into itself. That is, life is a self-fueling, self-sustaining, self-determining, and self-creating process. It depends on itself, relies on itself, and looks to itself to tell itself what the next expression of itself shall be.

This is true universally, it is true globally, it is true nationally, it is true locally, and it is true individually. It is merely a matter of proportion. And so we see the Universe deciding about itself in this way, our planet deciding about itself in this way, our nation deciding about itself in this way, our own city or community deciding about itself in this way, and our own *person* deciding about itself in this way. Life *informs* Life *about* Life *through the process of Life Itself.*

Life's information creates life in formation. At the most personal level, *your* information creates you, in formation. You are constantly forming and reforming yourself, shaping and reshaping yourself, creating and re-creating yourself anew. Indeed, the function of life is to re-create yourself anew in each golden moment of Now, in the next grandest version of the greatest vision ever you held about Who You Are.

> I don't know how a person advances in their evolution without giving some answer to these questions.

That's all of it, in a nutshell. That's what's going on here. All of humanity is engaged in this process. We are doing it politically, we are doing it economically, we are doing it culturally, we are doing it racially, we are doing it socially, we are doing it sexually, we are doing it spiritually. This is all we are doing *and we're not doing anything else.*

This is what *God* is doing. God is re-creating Itself anew in the single and only moment called Now—and life is God, *doing this.* Life is God, expressing Itself in an endless multiplicity of forms. You are one of the forms of God. You are, all of you, God's information. And thus, Gods... in formation.

POINTS I HOPE YOU WILL REMEMBER...

- The Seven Simple Questions are unsettling. That is their power.

- Revolutions are a way of life on this planet.

- One Final Revolution is all we will need to end such societal upheaval forever.

ACTION I HOPE YOU WILL TAKE...

- Read the Seven Simple Questions over and over until you can recite them verbatim.

- Ask yourself these questions and search deeply within your soul for your answers.

- Write your answers in a notebook, so that you may be very clear what your responses are, and so that you may refer to them over time—such as a year from now—to see what, if anything, has changed in your perceptions.

- Be prepared to offer the answers you have come up with as you explore these questions with others.

DON'T YOU THINK *SOMEONE* SHOULD BE TALKING ABOUT THIS?

OKAY, WE'RE ON OUR WAY. These questions are guaranteed to perk up ears in any group.

> Perk up ears is one thing. Change the world is another.
> Is that what this whole thing is all about? I've stuck with
> you all this way so that you could tell me to "Go out and
> have conversations about seven questions"? That's it? I
> sure was expecting more than that.

I don't blame you for having those thoughts. It *doesn't* seem like much of a solution to the problems at hand, does it? But can I tell you something?

It's *conversations,* little conversations, that start big revolutions. And we are talking here about The Conversation of the Century.

It's conversations that change people's minds and help people make *up* their minds. And conversations around these trenchant questions could ignite a global movement generating enormous social developments that really *could* change the world.

The impact of simple dialogue

Let me share something here from Margaret J. Wheatley, author of *Turning to One Another: Simple Conversations to Restore Hope to the Future* (2002).

This is a globally known consultant on organizational behavior. She received her doctorate from Harvard University, holds an M.A. in systems thinking from New York University, and has worked on every inhabited continent in virtually every type of organization.

In other words, Meg Wheatley knows her way around. Here's what she says:

"There is no more powerful way to initiate significant social change than to start a conversation."

Wow. I couldn't have *paid* her to say something better suited to make the point I've been making here. In a 2002 article in *Utne Reader,* Ms. Wheatley observes that "...true conversation is...a timeless and reliable way for humans to think together. Before there were classrooms, meetings or group facilitators, there were people sitting around talking.

"We can take courage from the fact that this is a process we all know how to do. We can also take courage in the fact that many people are longing to converse again. We are hungry for a chance to talk. People want to tell their stories, and are willing to listen to yours. We are awakening an ancient practice, a way of being gathered that all humans intimately understand.

> "There is no more powerful way to initiate significant social change than to start a conversation."

"Change doesn't happen from someone announcing the plan. Change begins from deep inside a system, when a few people notice something they will no longer tolerate, or when they respond to someone's dream of what's possible."

That is precisely, *to the letter,* what The Conversations Movement is all about.

You know something? We did that in the Sixties. We were very serious in those days. We were thinking of our children, we were concerned about the planet, we were doing sit-ins, we rallied together and marched, we were thinking seven generations ahead...and we talked and talked and talked. But it feels like we've actually gone backwards since then.

At least then we could *have* a conversation. Today it feels as if there's less tolerance, less acceptance, less willingness to even respectfully *listen* to an opposing point of view; more ugly

division, more demonizing by those who disagree. The "peace
and love" generation tried, and where did it get us?

There absolutely *is* more polarization in society today than ever
before. But that's the whole point being made here. What you did in the
Sixties *led* to this.

Oh, great. So it's our fault.

No, it's to your *credit*. You and many others in the Sixties generation
helped to bring about the End of an Era. Polarization is the natural result
of that. It is the signal that the era is actually *coming* to an end.

This ending of the era may not have happened as fast as you would
have liked 40 years ago, but make no mistake, that was the impetus that
got the snowball rolling downhill. And now we have an avalanche.

Eras have always ended with the emergence of the sharpest divisions
ever between one point of view and another, between yesterday's ideas
and tomorrow's hopes, because it is at the end of an era that those who
cannot let go of their Old Cultural Story feel the most threatened, and so
hold on most tightly.

So yes, many of us older folks did talk and talk in the Sixties. We
sat around in circles and gabbed our heads off, sometimes until the sun
came up. And thus began a 50-year shift in humanity's thinking.

It takes a long time to turn a big ship around. Humanity couldn't
have done it any faster, because it didn't have the tools of amplification
and the "glue-ification" we have today. We couldn't make our words
heard or stick.

We didn't have Facebook and Twitter and YouTube and MySpace.
We didn't have emailing and texting and Googling. That entire social networking apparatus was used in 2011 to amplify and "glueify" individual
conversations, resulting, as I have already noted, in the total changing of
the governments of entire countries. Such powerful and widespread acti-
vation and mobilization would have been utterly impossible in the Sixties.

But now our little conversations can get big; our community-based
conversations can go global. And we have even more people joining with
us. We have the younger ones. We have the folks in their 20s, 30s, and
40s. Now imagine *all of us* getting in on the act.

And imagine each person in community-based discussion groups going home, getting on their computer and sharing with their social networking community all that they've just heard and explored. Suddenly a conversation with four or six people can turn into a conversation with four or six *hundred*.

What we did in the Sixties was a good start. It was the "beginning of the beginning." But what is going on now *is* the Beginning—capital 'B.' We see this, we can feel the momentum, and so the goal of The Conversations Movement is to engage 250 million people in The Conversation of the Century within three to five years.

As I said, no reach on that scale could have been envisioned by anyone but major television networks and print media moguls in the Sixties. Today the power of mass communication has been harnessed by the masses themselves. And that is the difference.

Also, we didn't have the Seven Simple Questions.

> But do you really think that a simple invitation to have a conversation, even in this day and age of electronic connection, can draw 250 million people into a dialogue?

If Facebook can attract 500 million to talk about what they had for breakfast, half that number can surely be motivated to talk about things that actually *matter*.

All it will take to rewrite our Cultural Story is the reaching of critical mass in the energies around the idea. We have to reach a certain level in the number of people who are sufficiently interested in their own lives and in humanity's future to spend time exploring what we all believe, and then proposing what we *might* believe that could yield different results, given that we don't like the results we've produced so far.

I'm impressed with the words of the late Robert Kennedy: "And if our times are difficult and perplexing, so are they challenging and filled with opportunity," he said. "It is not enough to understand, or to see clearly...

"There are those who look at things the way they are and ask, Why?...I dream of things that never were and ask, Why not?"

> Instead of "exploring what we all believe," shouldn't we be *living* what we believe?

No. The problem is not that people have not been living what they believe. The problem is *that they have been.*

That's a pretty strong statement.

People hold some pretty strong beliefs. Chief among them…the belief that we are separate from God, that we are separate from each other, that there is "not enough" of what we need to be happy, that we have to compete with each other in order to get enough, or grow, grow, *grow the economy* in order to *produce* enough, and that there is something we all have to do to "earn" our right just to take up space on the planet, to speak our mind, to have our share, to give our gift—and most of all, to be with God in heaven.

> I dream of things that never were and ask, Why not?

And it all stems from those first two thoughts: that God is separate from us and that we are separate from each other.

Of course God is separate from us. What do you think, that God is the same as we are? Sorry, but it's *that* kind of muddled thinking that creates what you call the "problems in the world today."

(I had this actual conversation on talk radio recently. I responded…)
We seem to have a different view of who and what God is, you and I.

I'm sure that we do.

You think God is something outside of yourself, and I'm saying that God and you—God and all of us—are One. And I'm saying that the idea that God is separate from us is at the top of the list of Beliefs That Cause Humanity's Misery.

How? How does the belief that God is great, God is good, cause humanity misery?

I'm sorry. I didn't mean to suggest that God is not great or God is not good. I simply said God is not separate from us, or "other" than us.

> But that's the same as saying that God is *not* great, because if the way *we* are is the way *God* is, that doesn't sound very great to me.
> So are you telling me that this is as "great" and as "good" as God gets…is that it? God is not "other" than *us,* so *WE* are the "God" that we supposed to worship? That's a tough one. I don't think I can go there.

I believe that humans could experience themselves as being as great and as good as God is, if they only stopped telling themselves that they cannot.

> We cannot be as great and as good as God is. We simply cannot. That's just plain hubris.

I know you believe this, and I respect what you believe, but I'm wondering if it might not just be a matter of scale.

> I'm not following that. You lost me on that last turn.

Well, I understand that we cannot be as *large* as God; that would be impossible. A drop of the ocean is not the ocean.

> That's right.

But it is the *same* as the ocean, simply in a smaller portion. So the drop and the ocean are the same stuff. And *proportionate to its size*, the drop can be as great as the ocean. To a microscopic life form, the drop may as well *be* the ocean. So we're talking here about nothing more than *proportion.*

But let me ask you a question. What do you think this world would be like if we *did* "worship" other people as if they were God? Do you think we'd have more wars, or less? Do you think we'd have more arguments, more fights, more terror, more violence, or less?

That isn't the point.

It isn't? Then what is?

> The point is that the way to have less violence, fewer
> wars, and a better world is to *listen* to God and do what
> God says, not try to be God.
>   Humanity's problem is too much ego, not too little
> ego! You want us to run around thinking that we are God?
> Good grief.

Let me move in a different direction for a moment. I find myself
wanting to point out that many human beings are not happy. In fact,
most are not. We can agree on that, can we not?

> Yes, we can agree on that. The world's a mess.

And so we live in a society whose members are lashing out in frustration and anger, in defensiveness and bewilderment. They experience that
they live in a world that is constantly attacking them—or at the very
least, preventing them. It's stopping them from having what they want.
Most people do not see humanity as having had a role in creating the
world like that.

What we can do in the global conversations I'm suggesting is keep
talking about who we are and about the ability that we have to re-create
our world anew if we simply embrace the highest truth about who we are.

> If you're saying we should be talking about being
> "God," I'm not going to be able to get behind that. I can
> support trying to make the world a better place, but I can't
> support going around talking nonsense.

I appreciate you for being so clear. But you know, it was George
Bernard Shaw who famously observed, "All great truths begin as blas-
phemies." So I want to simply notice that most *every* new idea is going
to sound like nonsense to some people—especially if it's an idea about
us and God.

I know that what is being said here, that we are all Divine, runs counter to our present Cultural Story, our present understanding. It violates our values. It shakes us up. It even gets some of us mad. But I always look closely at the ideas that make me angry.

Anger is the first sign that I may be looking at something I don't want to look at; that I may be confronting something that challenges some pretty fundamental idea I hold. This is not always the case, but I've learned that it's true a lot of the time when somebody says something or proposes something that makes me angry.

So I don't walk away from an idea that makes me angry. I walk into it. I explore it. Maybe there's something there for me; maybe there's something for me to look at more closely. If not, what's the harm? If I've done nothing but reaffirm my prior belief and now hold it more closely, wouldn't that be a good thing?

> All great truths begin
> as blasphemies.

I'm proposing here that we not be afraid to talk a little "nonsense" now and then, because as part of our conversation around such thoughts, we can sometimes get to something that *is* "sense." Or…we can discover that the "nonsense" was not nonsense after all.

For instance, I want to suggest that part of humanity's problem right now is that it has a decidedly wrong set of priorities.

POINTS I HOPE YOU WILL REMEMBER…

- Little conversations start big revolutions.

- Change begins when a few people notice something they will no longer tolerate, or when they respond to someone's dream of what's possible.

- Sharply divided opinions, such as those we are seeing increasingly in the world today, are sure signs that an era is ending.

- Anger is a good indicator that there may be something for you to look at more closely.

ACTION I HOPE YOU WILL TAKE...

- Make a list of the last five opinions, comments, or ideas you can remember dramatically disagreeing with. Look at those comments or opinions again and see if there is anything important Life is trying to say to you around those subjects.

- Use Facebook, Twitter, YouTube, MySpace, and other social media to spread the word about The Global Conversation and its website at *www. TheGlobalConversation.com.*

A BRAND NEW PRIORITY FOR YOU . . . AND FOR HUMANITY

OKAY, LET'S TALK SOME more "nonsense." I just presented the Seven Simple Questions that I believe would, if asked at the right time in the right place, ignite conversations that could change our world's view of itself.

Now I know that there are some people who are not going to be interested in moving beyond the second question. You will recall, that question was...

> Is it possible
> that there is something
> we do not fully understand about life,
> *the understanding of which*
> *would change everything?*

If the majority of human beings say "no"—well, there's not much more for us to discuss. If most people believe that we as a species know everything right now that we need to know to create the lives that we wish to live, then exploration of new tools for the future will seem pointless.

We can all just drop these inquiries, go on living our lives moment-to-moment trying to get everything we want, working to give everyone we love what they want, hope for the best for ourselves, our children and their children, and let it go at that.

Yet I have a different proposal to make. I want to suggest that the trick is not to keep trying to get for ourselves, and give everyone else, what is wanted. The trick is to *change what is wanted.*

The trick is to set a brand new priority for ourselves.

Now if *that's* not enough to start a spritely conversation in your home and in your community, then nothing is. You might start the conversation by saying, "What do you think will happen if we all just changed what we want?"

> What do you mean, "Change what we want"?

I mean exactly that. I mean, change what it is that you want for yourself and what you want to give your loved ones.

> We shouldn't want peace, security....what did you
> have on that list before....?

Peace, security, opportunity, prosperity, happiness, and love.

> Yeah. We shouldn't want that?

No. Because if that's what you want, you're going to keep trying to produce that.

> No kidding.

Well as Dr. Phil would say, how's that been working for you? Yet if what you want is *something else*, and you produce *that*, then your *producing* of that will give you *this.*

> I'm sorry. What in the heck are you saying...?

I'm saying that we're going after the wrong thing. Most of us are trying to produce the wrong thing. And *this is what we don't understand... the understanding of which would change everything.*

When we decide to change what we want, when we decide to produce the far more beneficial thing, the natural outcome will be that we'll also have what we were hoping to create before.

I'm saying that these things that we all say as a species that we want are things we can have—but not very easily, not without a great deal of struggle, if we go about trying to get them the way we've been trying to get them.

> We're going after the wrong thing. Most of us are trying to produce the wrong thing.

I'm answering the question: How is it possible for an entire species to desire the same thing and be unable, after thousands of years of trying, to get it?

I'm saying it is possible that we have not been able to get it after thousands of years because we've been trying to get it *in a way that's not working.*

So what is a way that will work?

My thought about it is that the way that will work is not to want the things we've been wanting at all. Instead of seeking, and trying to create peace, prosperity, happiness and all the rest, seek and try to create something much larger...

Which would be?

A knowledge and an experience of your real self, of who you really are. Go after *that,* and all the rest will follow.

You've said a number of times here now that humans are Divine. Is that what you're getting at?

I can't give you personal knowledge of your own true identity. Yes, I've given you *my* answer, but my answer is not important; it's not relevant to you, *and it shouldn't be.* Only your answer should be relevant to you.

The problem is that in the past many of us—most of us—have embraced other people's answers as if they were our own. Yet each person must finally answer the question for him or her Self.

While I know what my answer is, I am here just opening people to the question. Yet as people open this inquiry, I encourage them to consider all of the Seven Simple Questions, not just this one, and to explore them one after the other, in order. Just as I have done.

> Okay, so I've got to ask you…how do you come to give us these answers? What makes you think that your answers are right?

(I hope that this *monoconvologue* has proven to be a good literary device, giving you an opportunity to see how you might respond when other people come to you with the same kinds of questions. For instance, the questions just above are two questions that I get a lot—and you may be asked them as well. I have always responded…)

Well, first of all I'm not saying that my answers *are* "right." I'm simply asking, "Can we all agree that the answers we've been given in the past have not worked? And can we all agree that it might be beneficial to search for new ones together?"

So I've tried hard to make it very clear that there are no "correct" answers to these questions. The answers that are correct for you are the answers that you give. (And you may give different answers at different times of your life, by the way!)

Yet I believe that if you wish to move forward in your own evolution, you must offer *some* answers. I'll be offering some of my own as our conversation here continues. If feels to me that we ignore these questions at our peril.

The world *has* ignored them, and *is* in peril. So I think the discussion is worthwhile.

> Perhaps, but what makes you think that you should lead it? I'm not trying to be antagonistic here, I'm just wondering—where are you coming from with all of this?

It's not so much where I'm coming from that you may wish to ponder, but where we're all *going*. Our planet and its people are in the process of evolving, and that process is speeding up. And if we're not careful, it's going to take us exactly where for centuries we've been heading.

Where I'm "coming from" in all of this is a genuine desire to help humanity evolve by getting us moving forward with The Conversation of the Century. I want to get a discussion going because I'm watching people who are dazed, sleepwalking.

I'm watching a world not seeming to know what to do next. I'm watching an entire species that appears to be mystified as to how to proceed from here.

No, it appears to be mystified about *more* than that. Our species seems to be unclear not only on how to *proceed* from here, but how we *got* here. And if we don't understand our past, we don't stand a good chance of understanding how to most beneficially create our future.

So in just a bit now, I'm going to give us a look at our past by sharing with you the basic elements of our Old Cultural Story. It's important for us to look at this.

See, what's happening now is that some of humanity is awakening, and more of humanity is about to be awakening, so I'd like to assist in that process.

I think that *many* people would like to do that. Many are feeling this same impulse: the impulse to assist. They just don't know how to do that, specifically. They don't know what kind of assistance they can offer.

I'm simply creating a vehicle with which they—we—can all do that. I'm offering The Conversations Movement and placing on the table a global discussion of a possible New Cultural Story.

I'm calling that discussion The Conversation of the Century. I'm placing it before the world at *TheGlobalConversation.com*. I see the whole thing as a beginning; as a way to get us started; as a means of moving the energy.

But now let me repeat that the ideas I talk about are not mine, but were given to me in *Conversations with God*. And they have helped me tremendously. How could I not pass them on if I say that we're all companions on the journey?

> I've got to tell you that many other people through-
> out human history have claimed that they were spoken to
> directly by God ... or that for some other reason they were
> qualified to lead us. I was hoping this exchange between us
> was going to be different from "religion" or "politics as usual."

Oh, it is. Believe me, it is. What makes it different—*totally* different—is that I'm not claiming that the ideas I'm presenting here are "the
best" ideas or "the only" ideas that can solve humanity's problems. But we
need to start somewhere, and I think that it needs to be somewhere *new*.

What I see is that as we try to solve our problems we keep coming from
the same place; we keep starting our thinking in the exact same spot: deep
within our Old Cultural Story. That's why we're not solving anything.

We're not solving anything because we're not *changing* anything. Like
hamsters on a wheel, we're running and running and getting nowhere.
We need to *get off the wheel.*

> We're not
> solving anything
> because we're
> not *changing*
> anything.

The idea of The Conversations Movement
is to do just that. It is not to put forward the
"End All" Ideas, it is to place before humanity
the "Beginning Of It All" Ideas!

We want to be able to look back in 100
years and say that this was the beginning of it all;
this was when we finally changed our approach;
this was when people from all over the world
said, *"Enough! What we're doing is not working! There's got to be another way."*

Our job now, our opportunity, our exciting task is to place before the
world a set of ideas from which a brand new discussion may begin. I'm
going to propose some of those ideas right here, in the conversations that
we're about to get to in this book.

Then readers from all over the planet can offer *their* thoughts and
their ideas. That's what the website's about. Soon, we'll have a global conversation going. It'll be the—

> —I know, I know. The "Conversation of the Century."

Yes! And it will offer humanity such a fresh new beginning, with
inspired input from people of every nation, that this new start will launch

a new era. In fact, *hey*, that's not a bad little *slogan* there. *A new start...to launch a new era.*

One idea, in particular, could do just that.

15 words that turn everything upside-down

Out of the 3,000 pages in the *Conversations with God* dialogues, one idea, in particular, jumped out at me. I knew as soon as I heard it that it was revolutionary. Utterly, completely revolutionary. It's what I call a Turn Around Idea. If adopted, it would turn everything, *everything*, around. Talk about giving us a new start!

Okay, I'll bite. What is it?

God invited—dared, actually—every minister, every priest, every rabbi, every ulama, every political party, every head of state, every corporate executive, every leader in every area of life, to stand behind every pulpit, every political convention podium, every lectern, every desk in every classroom, and share a New Gospel.

God also predicted that none of those people, *none of them*, would do it. Not a pope, not a president, not a prime minister, not a chief ulama, not a head of any political party, and certainly not a classroom teacher... *no one* would do it. Because this is not something that in our present society we would *dare* teach our children. It is not something we would *dare* tell our congregations. And it is not something we could even *imagine* putting in our political party's platform.

Well, for goodness sake, what is it that's such a show-stopper...?

It's two simple sentences, a mere 15 words. But if its message were embraced by the world, that world would be magnificently altered. The New Gospel proposed by *Conversations with God* is...

WE ARE ALL ONE.
OURS IS NOT A BETTER WAY, OURS IS MERELY ANOTHER WAY.

Okay.

Well.

Yes…well. That's interesting. Especially the last part. It's an interesting idea.

But if people or political parties or religions don't believe they have a better way, why bother offering it?

Is that a fair question? If people feel a deep conviction, shouldn't they speak out?

That's a *very* fair question. So let me answer it by saying that the problem with people speaking out their deepest convictions is not the speaking out itself, but the implied message that is often not-too-well hidden beneath those convictions—which is that they are *absolutely right; that their way is the best way.*

When I asked the same question you just asked me, you know what I received in the *CWG* dialogue? This…

"Because you can't have a 'better' religion, or a 'better' political party, or a 'better' economic system, does that mean you should not have any at all?

"Must you know that yours will be the 'better' picture before you pick up a brush and paint? Can it not be simply *another* picture? *Another* expression of beauty?

"Must a rose be 'better' than an iris in order to justify its existence?

"I tell you this: You are all flowers in the Garden of the Gods. Shall we turn the garden under because one is no more beautiful than another? You have done exactly that. And then you lament, 'where have all the flowers gone?'

"You are all notes in the Celestial Symphony. Shall we decline to play the music because one note is no more crucial than another?"

But we're talking about solving problems here. That's all very poetic, but we have to *implement* ideas, not just talk about them. And of course we want to implement the *best* idea. And if we think ours *is* the best, we have to be able to say that, don't we?

Well, certainly. Yet saying that you "think it is" is one thing, insisting on it is another. Will you excuse me for bringing a bit of old-fashioned wisdom here? My father used to tell me, "Son, two heads are better than one."

If people spoke from their conviction, yet allowed that they might not necessarily have *all* the answers or the *best* solutions, but simply said that they see the same *problems* that we all do, and if they made it clear that they are genuinely interested in opening a dialogue to see if *combining* ideas might produce terrific answers, then we'd have something helpful.

Yet if people speak from their conviction in a way that makes it clear they're totally convinced that what they believe is absolutely, positively, without-a-doubt *right*, about *everything,* then we have another matter altogether.

And if they treat your opinions, and your very person, not as if you simply hold a different opinion, but as if you're just plain ignorant— or worse yet, *evil*—then we have not just another matter; then we have another problem. We've *created* a problem in order to solve a problem.

And that's what's happening right now. It's the polarization that we talked about earlier. It's normal to the process of an era ending, but that doesn't mean we have to *go forward* in the same way. So the New Gospel is a different way of going forward.

What is being discussed *here*, in *this* conversation, is "another way" we might do things, "another way" of being human. Not the "only way," not the "best way," but "another way."

This is an exploration, not a declaration; an invitation, not a proclamation; a observation, not a notification. Our gentle observation is this: What we've been doing is no longer working. There's some doubt that it ever worked. And then we ask a gentle question: Is it necessary for us to continue with it?

I've gathered some great suggestions on how to *not* continue it— ideas that have emerged from many sources over the years—and I've put them in Part Two of this book. I hope you'll explore them with me.

But first, I think it is only fair that I answer the Seven Simple Questions, just the way I'm asking you to. Not that my answers are any more important than anyone else's (and certainly not any more "accurate" or "right"), but if I'm asking you to play, I've got to play. So my answers are next.

POINTS I HOPE YOU WILL REMEMBER...

- The way for humanity to make life work is to change what it wants.

- A knowledge and an experience of your real self is what it would be of great benefit to seek.

- We are not solving anything on the planet because we are not changing anything on the planet, in terms of who we think we are and how we think we should be functioning.

- There is a New Gospel that would change everything if we would simply embrace it.

ACTION I HOPE YOU WILL TAKE...

- Change what you want in life. Decide right now that it's not about safety or security or even happiness or prosperity or love. Decide that what you want is to truly know and experience yourself as who you really are.

- As you move through the world—and especially after you seek to know and express yourself as who you really are—remember and embrace the New Gospel. Repeat it often to others...and invite others to repeat it often to even more.

QUESTION #1:
ONE PERSON'S THOUGHTS

As I offer these responses to the Seven Simple Questions, I also want to model how I hope you'll begin offering _your_ answers. And remember these answers are only my answers. I'm pretty clear there are no "appropriate" or "right" answers to these questions, or responses that fit everyone. I can only share with you what I feel my soul saying to me.

Question #1

How is it possible for 6.9 billion people to all want the same thing—peace, happiness, abundance, opportunity, safety, security, and love—and be singularly unable to get it?

Some people have said this situation exists because not all people _do_ want the same thing. They've suggested that some people want revenge, or violence, or "their way" at all costs, and so forth.

I disagree with this. I believe that at the heart of every person, every person is wonderful. I believe that at the core of every human, every human desires not to hurt anyone else, ever, but that they sometimes do so anyway, out of a thought that they _can't_ have peace, happiness, abundance, opportunity, safety, security, and love.

They want all of these things just the way all of us do, but they feel that life, or some condition in life, is not allowing them to have them. So they become...how to put it...

. . . fighting mad.

This does not justify or condone actions that harm or destroy—but it does explain them. I believe that people who get fighting mad could be asked a single question that might defuse their anger, and the violent eruptions that too often spring from it.

Here's the question: "What hurts you so bad that you feel you have to hurt me in order to heal it?"

The power of this question is striking.

It is not true that some human beings are just "naturally evil." *Conversations with God* made this very clear to me. One of the dialogue's most compelling announcements was this: "No one does anything inappropriate, given their model of the world."

> How is it possible for 6.9 billion people to all want the same thing—peace, happiness, abundance, opportunity, safety, security, and love—and be singularly unable to get it?

How is it possible that an entire world full of people cannot get what they collectively insist they want? Simple. Their model of the world does not allow it.

I hate to keep harping on this, but the point must be made indelibly: The global population continues to embrace an ancient Cultural Story, a story based in primitive misunderstandings about life and God and who we are and what is "so" on this earth.

The majority of people have refused to let go of this story even though it has been proven to be not only *ineffective*, but actually *self-destructive*, as humanity has struggled for millennia to find a way to live in peace and harmony.

The world's people, having hung on to this old story tenaciously, believe and experience

> No one does anything inappropriate, given their model of the world.

that there is so much more they need in order to be happy. The point is made later in this conversation that there is enough of everything we need for all of us on the planet to be truly happy—all we have to do is find a way to share it. And what could *cause* us to share it would not be a new social system, but a new *belief* system.

POINTS I HOPE YOU WILL REMEMBER...

• At the heart of every person, every person is wonderful.

• No one does anything inappropriate, given their model of the world.

• The reason humanity cannot produce what it says it so desperately wants—peace, prosperity, security, goodwill, love, joy, fulfillment, and harmony—is because humanity's model of the world precludes it.

• The majority of people have refused to let go of this model even though it has been proven to be not only ineffective, but actually self-destructive.

• What is needed is not a new social system, but a new belief system; that is, a New Cultural Story.

ACTION I HOPE YOU WILL TAKE...

• On a sheet of paper, place the names of five people of your direct acquaintance that you have come to "not like so much" in your life. For each of these five people, write down five things that prove the statement that "every person is wonderful" at their core.

• Actually do the above little exercise. It will make you feel incredible, by allowing you to notice how much of what is really good in another you are actually able to see and acknowledge once you get your judgment even just a little out of the way.

- Test out the notion that "no one does anything inappropriate, given their model of the world." Write down three things that you have done in your own life that were judged by others to be "inappropriate." Leave a space after each one, so that you can add something later. Then, look closely at the model of the world you were holding at the time of each "infraction" that, in each case, allowed you to go ahead and do what you did. Write this down.

- The next time others damage you or ruffle your feelings in any way, try to remember to ask them, "What hurts you so bad that you feel you have to hurt me in order to heal it?"

QUESTION #2:
ONE PERSON'S THOUGHTS

THE SECOND OF THE Seven Simple Questions always seems rhetorical to me. Humanity's intelligent response to the question can only be *yes*. I mean, if the response genuinely, truly, and really is *no,* then human beings are in much more trouble than any of us thought.

Question #2

Is it possible that there is something we don't fully understand about God and about life, the understanding of which would change everything?

Of course it's possible, and it's what is so. To declare that we understand everything about God and life is sheer folly.

Clearly, there is an information gap here. Clearly, all the data is not in. Yet some people believe that we have all the information we need to live a complete and fruitful life. It's found in The Holy Scriptures.

Yet which Holy Scriptures? Which book contains the One and Only True Word of God?

Well, now that depends upon to whom one is speaking. Many say, the New Testament. Others say, no, God's word is found in the Hebrew Bible. Others say, no, His word is found in the Qur'an.

Others say, no, it's in the Torah.

Others say, no, in the Mishna.

Others say, the Talmud.

Others, the Bhagavad-gita.

Others, the Rig Veda.

Others, the Brahmanas.

Others, the Upanishads.

Others, the Mahabharta and the Ramayana.

Others, the Puranas.

Others, the Tantras.

Others, the Tao-te Ching.

Others, the Buddha-Dharma.

Others, the Dhammapada.

Others, The Master of Huai-nan.

Others, the Shih-chi.

Others, the Pali Canon.

Others, the Book of Mormon.

Others...

Well, the point is, many people believe that Direct Revelation—that is, God speaking directly to Man—is found in the Holy Scriptures with which *they feel most comfortable.*

This makes it a little bit difficult for humans to find out what it is they may not fully understand about God and about life, because the words found in books other than those of our own spiritual tradition are considered to be inaccurate.

And books such as *Conversations with God?* Now you're talking blasphemy. You see, the world's religions agree wholeheartedly that God speaks directly to human beings—after all, God spoke directly to the human beings who were considered to be the *source* of those religions (Moses, Jesus, Muhammad, Baha'u'llah, Joseph Smith, etc.)—and they also agree, whatever other differences exist between them, that God has not spoken directly to human beings *lately.*

> Is it possible that there is something we don't fully understand about God and about life, the understanding of which would change everything?

Since speaking directly to the source of *their* religion, the faithful declare, God has come down with a very bad case of celestial laryngitis. No more speaking directly to humans is being done.

So here's the rule of thumb: If it's an Old Book, produced from the inspiration of God as given to Man hundreds or thousands of years ago, there's at least a chance that it may be true. If it's a New Book, produced from the inspirations of God given to Humanity *today,* there's *no chance in heaven* that it's anything but blasphemy.

Old is good, old is God; new is bad, new is blasphemy. Got it?

What we don't know

Still, none of this is problematical, right? Because we know all that we need know, yes? We know enough to be able to create the collective and individual life of which humanity has long dreamed, do we not?

No, we do not. There is still something we do not fully understand... the understanding of which would change everything.

When I was a young man there was a saying: "What you don't know won't hurt you." Today it is exactly the opposite. What you don't know *will* hurt you.

What we don't know about God and about life is plentiful—and it's killing us.

We don't understand who and what God is, we don't understand God's desire (even though every religion says it does), we don't understand how God functions or interacts with the world (if, indeed, God does), and we don't understand our true relationship with God.

Why does God say "yes" to some people and "no" to others? Why does God say "no" today to the people He said "yes" to yesterday? Why does God allow bad things to happen to good people? Why does God.... why, why, *why....???*

While the world's religions have sought genuinely to bring us as much insight as possible on the one hand, it has regretfully stifled continued questioning and exploration on the other.

And so, if we do not accept the now centuries-old answers we've been given (and we *should* not—look where they've gotten us!), we're pretty much left to our own devices as we seek to know God more fully; and to experience life more peacefully, harmoniously, and happily.

> There's something missing here. There's obviously some data missing.

There's something missing here. There's obviously some data miss-ing. But it takes such courage to admit even *that*, much less to offer some suggestions on what the missing data may *be*, that the question has effectively been closed for most religions—and therefore, by extension, for most of humanity.

Not for all of it, mind you. But for most of it.

So here is the irony: While a very large number of people would readily admit that we don't, on this earth, fully understand God and life, the pursuit of newer understandings is deeply discouraged, if not roundly denounced.

And to most people the idea that one person or two, a small collec-tion or a little group here or there, may in fact have come to discover something *more*, or *new*, is absolute anathema. Totally unacceptable.

We will not be "one upped" by anyone—even if it puts all of us one down.

What we don't know

And it is not just all the stuff around "God" that we don't under-stand. We don't know half of what we need to know to truly understand life itself, *exclusive* of the experience of our various Deities.

We don't understand even the rudimentary elements or functions of Life Energy. We simply don't know how it works. We don't understand the magnetic qualities of attraction. We don't understand the power of fear. We do not and cannot seem to behold the miracle of love. I mean, true love. Unconditional love.

We insist that if something can't be measured, analyzed, tested, and proven by scientific methods, it does not exist. We therefore eliminate from our own good use anything and everything having to do with extrasensory perception, mind fields, creative imagery, psychic insight, dream work, positive thinking, or any other nonmeasurable, inexpli-cable phenomena.

Let me give you just one tiny, tiny example of what I am talking about.

Let us say that you experience yourself wanting something desper-ately. Did you know that if you keep saying to yourself *I want that!*, you are announcing to the universe that you do not now have it? *And that this announcement produces your continuing reality?*

As long as you hold such a thought, you *cannot* have what you "want," because you cannot have on the one hand what you are confirming on the other that you do not. The point: Your Word Has Creative Power.

For instance, the statement "I want more money" may not draw money to you, but may actually push it away. This is because the universe has only one response in its vocabulary: "Yes."

It listens to you very carefully, and it listens most of all to *what you are feeling*. The opening book in the *Conversations with God* series says that "feeling is the language of the soul." If you constantly say, "I want more money!" and the Universe "feels your feeling" around that, and it is a feeling of lack, *this is what the universe will respond to.*

The Engine of Creation is actually a magnet. We are talking about power here. The power of a magnet. Remember that a feeling is energy, and in the matter of energy, Like Attracts Like.

So the Universe will say "Yes!"—and you will continue *wanting more money*. If you think, "I want more love in my life!" . . . the universe will say "Yes!"—and you will continue *wanting more love in your life*.

In using the energy of life, the word "I" is the ignition key of creation. What follows the word "I" *turns* the key and starts the engine of manifestation. Thus, when it "looks as if" Personal Creation is not working, it is only because the Energy of Attraction has brought you what you *inadvertently selected* rather than what you thought you chose.

This is what is going on all over the world right now.

This is what has caused The Storm Before the Calm.

The power of life's energy is always ON. If it were not, if the process was not always working, you could have a single very positive thought about something

> The Engine of Creation is actually a magnet.

and that outcome would be made manifest in your reality without fail. But the process works all the time, not just part of the time, and is fed by that which you feel most deeply, most consistently.

So a single very positive thought in a whirlwind of not-so-positive ideas and projections is not likely to produce the desired result. The trick is to stay positive in a sea of negativity. The trick is to know that the process is working even when it *looks* as *if* it is not.

That is what we are talking about right here, in this conversation. That is what will turn this storm front around.

Yet much to our loss, humanity dismisses some of the most important and powerful aspects of life, such as how to understand and utilize life's energy. I have given you just one example above.

So...is there something we do not understand about God and about life? Of course there is.

Would it change everything if we understood it? Of course it would.

Does it make complete and total sense for humanity to have a conversation about this? Of course it does.

POINTS I HOPE YOU WILL REMEMBER...

- There is an information gap between what we know and what we need to know about God and Life.

- That information gap is huge, it is not small.

- If we began to close this gap, it would change everything.

ACTION I HOPE YOU WILL TAKE...

- Make a list—yes, an actual list—of Things I Know about God. See how this lines up with what you were taught as a child or came to understand through the common culture.

- Make a list—yes, an actual list—of Things I Know about Life. See how this lines up with what you were taught as a child or came to understand through the common culture.

- Learn all you can about the energy of life and how it works. Promise yourself to actually make a study of it in the next year. Twelve months from today, add this to your discussions with others about the Seven Simple Questions.

QUESTION #3:
ONE PERSON'S THOUGHTS

ALWAYS THE TOUGHEST AND most significant questions get back to us, to ourselves, to that person in the mirror. We can externalize life all we want to as long as we want, but at the end of the day, when the head hits the pillow, it comes down once again to The One Behind the Closed Eyes.

Question 3

Is it possible that there is something we do not fully understand about *ourselves,* about our own life and its purpose, *the understanding of which would shift our reality and alter our experience for the better, forever?*

Of course it's possible, and it's what is so. We hardly understand anything about ourselves. We don't even understand how we think, or why we think the way we think.

We don't understand who we are or where we are or how we got here or why in the heck we *are* here anyway.

We don't understand our relationship to God, our relationship to each other, our purpose in life and…most regrettable of all…we don't understand how to love.

Most of us don't even know what love *is.*

We don't understand why things happen in our life the way they do, and we don't understand how to cope with them *when* they do. We are completely at a loss to explain most of what's going on around us—and even if we do have an explanation, we don't understand how to make practical use of it, how to live it.

These observations, by the way, have applied to me. That is why I can offer this answer with such articulation. I am very clear that I have not understood, and that there is still so much, much more to understand.

I did not understand until I turned 50 that the entire purpose of my life was to re-create myself anew in the next grandest version of the greatest vision ever I held about Who I Am. I did not know that every act is an act of self-definition.

When I asked God, in my moment of earnest and deep yearning, why my life was not working, God said, "That's easy. You think your life is about you."

I was made to understand that my life had nothing to do with me, but rather, with everyone whose life I touched—and with how I touched them. I wished someone had told me this 30 years earlier....

> *Is it possible that there is something we do not fully understand about ourselves, about our own life and its purpose, the understanding of which would shift our reality and alter our experience for the better, forever?*

I didn't know that I was holy. A sacred aspect of The Sacred Itself. I thought I was nothing, smaller than a piece of dust in the cosmic sky. Then I discovered Who I Really Am—who we *all* are—and what we are all doing here, and everything shifted in my life.

I found that earlier in my life I knew *nothing* of the real truths of life. I thought it was about get the car, get the girl, get a job, get the diploma, get the spouse, get the kids, get the house, get the raise, get the better car, get the better job, get the bigger house, get the gray hair, get the grandkids, get the office on the top floor in the corner, get the retirement watch, get the pension, get the cruise tickets, get the apartment that replaces the house, get the illness, get the sympathy, and get the hell out.

I mean, *that's what I thought life was all about.*

Late in life I learned that I was here on Earth on a divine mission, serving the purpose of the soul, and that I had spent 98% of my time on the 98% of things that simply didn't matter.

Now I know better. As my father used to say, "So old so soon, so smart so late." And as my mother used to say, "Better late than never."

Are there things that most of us do not understand about ourselves and about who we are, the understanding of which would alter our lives forever for the better? Of course there are.

POINTS I HOPE YOU WILL REMEMBER...

- We hardly understand anything about ourselves.

- We don't understand our relationship to God, our relationship to each other, our purpose in life and... most regrettable of all...we don't understand how to love.

- When we understand these things, our whole world changes; our life is never again the same.

ACTION I HOPE YOU WILL TAKE...

- Undertake the work of the soul. Determine this moment to begin spending 20 minutes a day with your soul. Use the guidelines toward the end of this book as a means of creating that experience, or any other tools that you wish, but promise yourself to do it.

QUESTION #4:
ONE PERSON'S THOUGHTS

SOONER OR LATER IN our lives we have to make a major decision about the most important question in life: What is our actual identity? Are we the physical manifestation of a biological incident, or are we something greater, something more, something other than a mere mammal?

Question 4

Who are you?

As I observe it, I have a couple of choices when it comes to how I think of myself. I also observe that *there is no "right way" to answer this question.*

Choice #1: I could conceive of myself as a Chemical Creature, a "Logical Biological Incident." That is, the logical outcome of a biological process engaged in by two older biological processes called my mother and my father.

If I see myself as a Chemical Creature, I would see myself as having no more connection to the Larger Processes of Life than any other chemical or biological life form.

Like all the others, I would be impacted *by* life, but could have very little impact *on* life. I certainly couldn't create events, except in the most remote, indirect sense. I could create more *life* (all chemical creatures carry the biological capacity to re-create more of themselves), but I could not create what life *does*, or how it "shows up" in any given moment.

Further, as a Chemical Creature I would see myself as having a very limited ability to create an intentioned *response* to the events and conditions of life. I would see myself as a creature of habit and instinct, with only those resources that my biology brings me.

I would see myself as having more resources than a turtle, because my biology has gifted me with more. I would see myself as having more resources than a butterfly, because my biology has gifted me with more.

I would see myself as having more resources than an ape or a dolphin (but, in those cases, perhaps not all that *many* more), because my biology has gifted me with more. Yet that is all I would see myself as having in terms of resources.

I would see myself as having to deal with life day-by-day pretty much as it comes, with perhaps a tiny bit of what seems like "control" based on advance planning, etc., but I would know that at any minute anything could go wrong—and often would.

Another option

Choice #2: I could conceive of myself as a Spiritual Being inhabiting a biological mass—what I call a "body."

If I saw myself as a Spiritual Being, I would see myself as having powers and abilities far beyond those of a simple Chemical Creature—powers that transcend basic physicality and its laws.

I would understand that these powers and abilities give me collaborative control over the *exterior* elements of my Individual and Collective Life and complete control over the *interior* elements—which means that I have total ability to create my own reality, because my reality has nothing to do with *producing* the exterior elements of my life and everything to do with how I *respond to* the elements that have been produced.

> My purpose has to do with my *interior* life.

Also, as a Spiritual Being, I would know that I am here (on the earth, that is) for a spiritual reason. This is a highly focused purpose and has little to do directly with my occupation or career, my income or possessions or achievements or place in society, or *any* of the exterior conditions or circumstances of my life.

I would know that my purpose has to do with my *interior* life—and that how well I do in *achieving* my purpose may very often have an *effect* on my exterior life.

(For the interior life of each individual cumulatively produces the exterior

Who are you?

life of the collective. That is, those people around you, and those people who are around those people who are around you. It is in this way that you, as a Spiritual Being, participate in the evolution of your species.)

My decision

My answer to Question #4: I've decided that I am a Spiritual Being, a three-part being made up of Body, Mind, and Soul. Each part of my tri-part being has a function and a purpose. As I come to understand each of those functions, each aspect of me begins to more efficiently serve its purpose in my life.

I am an individuation of Divinity, an expression of God, a singularization of The Singularity. There is no separation between me and God, nor is their any difference, except as to proportion. Put simply, God and I are one.

This brings up an interesting question. Am I rightly accused of heresy? Are people who believe that they are divine nothing but raving lunatics? Are they, worse yet, apostates?

I wondered. So I did a little research. I wanted to find out what religious and spiritual sources had to say on the subject. Here's some of what I found…

Isaiah 41:23—Shew the things that are to come hereafter, that we may know that ye are gods: yea, do good, or do evil, that we may be dismayed, and behold together.

Psalm 82:6—I have said, 'Gods ye are, And sons of the Most High—all of you.'

John 10:34—Jesus answered them, Is it not written in your law, I said, Ye are gods?

The Indian philosopher Adi Shankara (788 CE—820 CE), the one largely responsible for the initial expounding and consolidation of Advaita Vedanta, wrote in his famous work, *Vivekachudamant:* "Brahman is the only Truth, the spatio-temporal world is an illusion, and there is ultimately Brahman and individual self."

Sri Swami Krishnananda Saraswati Maharaj (April 25, 1922—November 23, 2001), a Hindu saint: "God exists; there is only one God; the essence of man is God."

According to Buddhism, there ultimately is no such thing as a self independent from the rest of the universe (the doctrine of anatta). Also, if I understand certain Buddhist schools of thought correctly, humans return to Earth in subsequent lifetimes in one of six forms, the last of which are called Devas...which is variously translated as *Gods* or *Deities*.

Meanwhile, the ancient Chinese discipline of Taoism speaks of embodiment and pragmatism, engaging practice to *actualize the Natural Order within themselves*. Taoists believe that man is a microcosm for the universe.

Hermeticism is a set of philosophical and religious beliefs or gnosis based primarily upon the Hellenistic Egyptian pseudepigraphical writings attributed to Hermes Trismegistus. Hermeticism teaches that there is a transcendent God, The All, or one "Cause," of which we, and the entire universe, participate.

The concept was first laid out in *The Emerald Tablet of Hermes Trismegistus*, in the famous words: "That which is Below corresponds to that which is Above, and that which is Above, corresponds to that which is Below, to accomplish the miracles of the One Thing."

And in Sufism, an esoteric form of Islam, the teaching *There is no God but God* was long ago changed to *There is nothing but God*. Which would make me...well...*God*.

Enough? Do you wish or need more? You might find it instructive and fascinating to go to *Wikipedia*, the source to which I owe my appreciation for much of the above information.

As well, read the remarkable books of Huston Smith, 91 years of age at this writing and a globally honored professor of religion. Among titles of his that I most often recommend: *The World's Religions: Our Great Wisdom Traditions*, 1958, rev. ed. 1991, HarperOne; and *Forgotten Truth: The Common Vision of the World's Religions*, 1976, reprint ed. 1992, HarperOne.

So...that is my answer to the fourth question. I am an out-picturing of the Divine. I am God in human form. So, too, of course, are we all.

POINTS I HOPE YOU WILL REMEMBER...

• The question of who you are is the most important question of your life.

• There is no "right way" to answer the question.

• You have a couple of choices when it comes to how you think of yourself.

ACTION I HOPE YOU WILL TAKE...

• Look at this question deeply. Not once, but every day, first thing in the morning and last thing at night, for one year solid. Look at the question and give yourself the answer that feels true for you in that moment. Do not tailor the answer to what you think an enlightened being would say. Let your answer be your truth.

• Give yourself permission to move your conversation with others into this important area. After discussing the Three Persistent Questions, gently invite the exploration into a look at this most profound inquiry. See the final of the Seven Simple Questions for brief hints on how to hold a Seven Questions Discussion Group.

Conversation #14

QUESTION #5, 6, AND 7: ONE PERSON'S THOUGHTS

My answers to the last three questions came all in a rush for me, so I'm going to include them all in a single conversation.

Question 5

Where am I?

My answer is that I am on the Eternal Journey of the Soul. I am moving on that journey from the Realm of the Spiritual to the Realm of the Physical to the Realm of the Virtual in a continuing cycle.

The Realm of the Spiritual is the realm of the absolute, where everything exists in its absolute state. In this realm there is only Love, it is always Now, and there is only Here. This state of Always Here/Now/Love has sometimes been called Heaven. In truth, it is but a part of heaven. One of three aspects or expressions in "paradise." ("In my Kingdom there are many mansions.")

This realm may also be called the Realm of Knowing, because everything that is, is utterly and completely known.

The Realm of the Physical is the realm of the relative, where things exist relative to other things. Here there is up and down, big and small, fast and slow, hot and cold, here and there, before and after, male and female, and an entire universe of what appear to be dualities (but are really triads—more on this later!).

This realm may also be called the Realm of Experiencing, because the soul places itself here in order to experience, in relative terms, what it knows itself to be absolutely.

The Realm of the Virtual is the realm of virtually everything/always. It is what we would call, in today's technological terms, a Virtual Reality. That is, exactly as on a computer, we are *making it all up.*

God is the Great Maker-Upper. Or, if you prefer more respectful and reverent language…God is the Creator.

This realm is the place of Pure Being, where That Which Is resides in its Isness. This is the place of the All-in-All, the Whole of Everything, the Power and the Glory, the Sum Total.

This realm may also be called the Realm of Being.

My current location

I am, right now, in the Realm of the Physical. This is not a way-station outside of heaven, where I work in some way to make myself "worthy" of returning to God.

Nor it is a school, where I must make passing grades. There is nothing for me to learn, there is only for me to remember. Everything I needed to know I knew when I arrived here. It is part of my cellular encoding.

The 300-year-old tree outside my window knows nothing more now

> Where am I?

about how to be a tree than it knew when it was a seedling, no bigger than the nail on my little finger. All it has done is grow into itself, becoming more of what it always was.

I am doing precisely the same thing.

Nor is this place where I am a testing ground, where I am put through my paces to make sure I am up to snuff. I was perfect when I arrived here, I am perfect in this moment, and I will ever and always be perfect through the entirety of my eternal and everlasting life.

This place called Earth is simply (and magnificently) a place where I am able, because of its relative environment, to experience in lifetime after lifetime any and every aspect of God that it brings me joy to express in me, through me, as me.

There is nothing I have to do, nowhere I have to go, and no way I have to be except exactly the way I am being right now. My happiness is knowing this, my joy is expressing it, my bliss is experiencing it.

There's no journey, really

These three realms—this whole construction, if you will—was given to me in my conversations with God. There is obviously much more to explain about all of this. I am skimming the surface here, because to go much deeper would be to fill two books. I went this far because I felt it was only fair to offer the answers to these questions that have emerged through me and in me as a result of my own soul searching—and my direct questioning of God.

Not everyone would come up with the same answers even if they, too, questioned God. I am clear that God speaks to each of us in the language and using the terms and offering the analogies and illustrations that God knows will best allow us to understand with our finite minds the infinite reality.

If you would like more of what I was given about the realms visited on the journey of the soul, I invite you to read my books *HOME WITH GOD in a Life That Never Ends* and *When Everything Changes, Change Everything.*

For now, let me end my answer to question #5 with this: We are not really journeying anywhere. There is nowhere to go in the Kingdom, as it is always Now/Here. The illusion of "movement" from one "realm" to another, throughout the EverMoment that we call eternity, is the result of the placing of our attention on one part or another of that which is Always Present.

Yet even the placing of attention implies the existence of time, because the placing of attention on this or that appears to be a sequential activity. I assure you, however, that there is no such thing as Time as we commonly understand it, and that we have all of our attention on all of our creation in all of the spaces of All Of It all the time.

"Words," says *Conversations with God*, "are the least reliable form of communication," and this is never more true than when trying to explain the macro reality in micro terms.

Question 6

Why am I where I am?

My thought is that I am in the Realm of the Physical, or what may also be called the Realm of the Relative, because I desire a Contextual Field within which to Experience what I Know of myself, and to experience it fully.

I cannot experience who I am in the Realm of the Spiritual because there, there is nothing I am not. And in the absence of what I am not, what I am…is not. That is, it is not *experienceable*. You cannot experience What You Are *except* in the presence of What You Are Not.

The light cannot be experienced without the darkness. "Up" has no meaning in experience without "down." "Fast" is simply a term, a word, having no meaning whatsoever, without "slow."

Only in the presence of the thing called Small can the thing called Big be experienced. We can *say* that something is "big," we can *imagine* that something is "big," we can *conceptualize* something as being "big," but in the absence of something that is "small," "big" cannot be experienced.

Likewise, in the absence of something "finite," "infinity" cannot be experienced. Put into theological terms, in the absence of something that is "not God," the thing called "God" cannot be experienced. We can know "divinity" *conceptually*, but we cannot know it *experientially*.

Therefore, all the people, places, and events of your life—now or in the past—which seem to be "at odds" with who you are and what you choose to experience are simply gifts from the highest source, created for you and brought to you through the collaborative process of co-creating souls, allowing you to find yourself in a contextual field within which the fullest experience of Who You Really Are becomes possible.

Or to put this as God put it to me, "I have sent you nothing but angels." (A statement I never forgot.)

The cycle of my eternal journey, from the Realm of the Virtual to the Realm of the Spiritual to the Realm of the Physical, then returning to the Realm of Virtual, where the cycle begins all over again, has a purpose. It is important for me to know this, lest I think that I am on an endless merry-go-round.

The purpose of the Cycle of Life is to expand the Reality of God.

In simple terms (and these *are* simple terms), God is growing—becoming more of Itself—through this process. God IS this process. That is, God is the Process Itself...and the result of it. Thus, God is The Creator and The Created. The Alpha and the Omega. The Beginning and The End. The Unmoved Mover. The Unwatched Watcher.

In not-so-simple terms, God cannot "grow" because everything God ever was, is now, or ever will be Is Now. There is no Time and there is no Space. Therefore, there is no time in which to grow, and no space *into* which to grow. The Cycle of Life is therefore occurring simultaneously everywhere. What my human mind wants to call God's "growth" is merely God's experiencing more and more of Itself as God's individuations experience more and more of *them*selves. This is called Evolution.

By the unique, elegant, and remarkably simple invention of Individuation, God made it possible for the Always All and the Everything Now to experience Itself in a way that could make "growth" possible.

Stated simply, this was accomplished by The Whole by dividing but not separating itself from Itself, re-creating Itself in smaller and finite form. No finite form—by the very reason of its being finite—could hold the infinite consciousness, awareness, and experience of The Whole, yet each individuated Self was designed in such a way that what we call "expansion" of consciousness, awareness, and experience to a place where it once again equaled that of The Whole was possible through a process by which the individuated aspect did not *grow*, actually, but simply became more and more *aware* that it did not *have* to grow, but actually was, in its individuated form, identical to The Whole.

The story is there, the unfoldment is awaited

Let me see if I can illustrate this. Hold a DVD of your favorite movie in your hand. Notice that *the entire movie* exists on the disc. When you put the DVD into a player and watch the story unfold, you know at some level that everything has already happened. The disc isn't creating the story as it goes along, it is simply accessing the story, it is simply projecting a minuscule portion of *what is all there in whole and complete form*, onto your computer or television screen frame by frame.

When you hit Fast Forward, you can actually watch this process of accessing the story unfold rapidly, no longer in real time (as you understand "real time").

That's as close as I can come to explaining what is going on in your life and mine. Everything that ever was, is now, and ever will be…*is now.* The universe is the Original Disc. It is one of many in God's hands.…

Don't believe it? Fair enough. My answer may not be yours. But I am intrigued by this from Shakespeare:

There are more things in heaven and earth, Horatio, than are dreamt of in your philosophy. (Hamlet, Act I, Scene 5)

Question 7

What do I intend to do about that?

My idea is that I intend to keep myself aware that I am engaging in the Process of God. God is a Process. You are engaged in that Process now. I have always been, and I always will be.

This is Nirvana, this is Pure be Bliss. For Pure Bliss is the process of God "godding." If people do not experience life in this way, it is because they do not Know Who They Are, Where They Are, Why They Are Where They Are, or What They Intend to Do about That.

> God is a Process. You are engaged in that Process now.

Here in the Realm of the Physical I am producing and then living within a Contextual Field in order that Experience may occur. What Experience? The Experience I choose.

I make this choice by my co-creation of, and my response to, the Contextual Field, and my decision with regard to it. Within the Contextual Field I can React, Create, or Intend. It is up to me.

The process by which I experience what I came to physicality to experience is a process of increasing my awareness of the Process Itself. As I become more and more aware, I move from Reaction to Creation to Intention to Expression.

The Neophyte reacts. The Student creates. The Master intends. The Divine expresses.

Life in the Realm of the Physical invites me to Know, and to Know That I Know. It invites me to Master the

> What do I intend to do about that?

Moment. I can do this by moving into each moment deciding ahead of time what I Intend to Express.

I am inviting myself not to live my life as an experience of reaction, nor even as an experience of creation, but as an experience of intention, producing the expression of Divinity. This is what I call fulfillment.

In truth I cannot create anything, because everything has already been created. I am wasting my time trying to create something. That's child's play. When I am trying to create peace, security, opportunity, prosperity, happiness, and love, I am in the sandbox, playing with toys. I did not come here for that.

> The Neophyte reacts. The Student creates. The Master intends. The Divine expresses.

I came here to experience my Self as Who I Really Am; to express through me, as me, an aspect of Divinity—and to re-create myself anew in the next grandest version of the greatest vision ever I held about Who I Am.

When I do that, all those other things I was trying to produce in my life come to me without effort.

I could, of course, be wrong about all of this. But my experience has shown otherwise—and I have not found a more inspiring or a more exciting way to live.

POINTS I HOPE YOU WILL REMEMBER...

- There are three realms in the Kingdom of God.

- We are now in the Realm of the Physical.

- We are not here to learn anything, or to be tested.

- We are here to experience any aspect of Divinity that we wish. That is what makes this a paradise.

- You cannot experience What You Are except in the presence of What You Are Not.

- God is a process, and you are part of that process right now.

ACTION I HOPE YOU WILL TAKE...

- Completely rearrange your thinking about this place called Earth. Begin to experience life "on Earth as it is in heaven." That is, as if this were a paradise.

- In order to do this, you would have to rearrange your thinking about Who You Are and about How Life Works. You would have to adopt a new perspective—the perspective of the soul, on why things are happening the way they are happening, what the purpose of every event is, and how we can put those events to that purpose in a meaningful way.

- Make a list of conditions, experiences, and circumstances that have existed or now exist in your life that create a context allowing you to experience who you are by presenting you with who and what you are not. Bless those experiences and circumstances and forgive yourself for ever having made them wrong, or not okay with you (if, in fact, you ever did). Embrace them now in your heart as the gifts that each of them were and are.

"OH, MY DARLIN' CLEMENTINE..."

I THINK YOU'RE GOING to like some of the ideas about how we might collectively create our future; ideas that I believe God inspired. But I've not come here to simply post a *notification* to humanity of what is best for us and what we are now expected to do.

> But if you believe that you really did receive these ideas from God, why would you not want to make them a 'notification'?
> I could understand your modesty or your reluctance if you felt that these were your ideas…but is it your notion that God's thoughts about life and how to make it work are not good enough to simply be laid down as dictums? And if they truly came from God, should they not be dictums?

No. First, God does not lay down dictums. That would violate the first condition of life, which is Freedom. Or, as some religions have labeled it: Free Choice.

Freedom is a fundamental condition, it is an *Isness*, which God never would or could overrule or dismiss. God cannot overrule an *Isness* because God *Is* the *Isness*. The *Isness* will not and does not and cannot "un-Is" itself.

God IS Freedom—the perfect expression of that. So the *last* thing God could or would do is demand something or require something or force something. God, by God's very *nature*, could never be a dictator.

Second—to answer the question as it directly relates to me, personally—if I were trying to inspire humanity to seriously consider the ideas I've placed here by *using* its Free Choice, the last thing I would do would be to insist that these ideas are Right or Best—even if I do believe they came directly from God.

> God does not lay
> down dictums.

The very reason that most of the ideas that most of the religions have put into most the world have not worked is that most of those religions have declared most of their ideas to be Right and Best.

Nothing stops humanity from adopting an idea faster than being told that the idea dare not be opposed, because it is Right and Best.

The fascinating thing about humanity is that *we want to figure things out for ourselves,* we don't want to have someone else telling us what to do.

> But be honest. Don't you want humanity to adopt
> your ideas?

They're not my ideas.

> Okay, okay—what you claim to be God's ideas. Don't you
> want humanity to adopt them? Don't you believe in them?

I believe in them, I assure you, or I wouldn't be putting them out there. But the fact that I believe in them does not translate in my mind into a requirement that *you* should believe in them. This is the problem with most religions.

> But if you don't feel that I should adopt these ideas,
> why bother us with them? Why propose them? I'm right
> back to the original question.

So then let me go right back to my original answer. I'll try to find different words.

The purpose of proposing of an idea should be simply that. To propose it, not to *impose* it. There's a vast difference between *proposition* and *imposition*.

The difficulty with many of the world's religions and so many of their followers (and many political parties, too, for that matter) is that they too often seek to *impose their views on others.*

If they simply *proposed* rather than *imposed*, there would be no problem. There also would not have been the Crusades, the jihads, the ethnic cleansings, and the countless other horror-ridden and totally unacceptable tactics by means of which, throughout history, one group has sought to overlay its views and ideas on another.

Right now there do tend to emerge certain "litmus tests" that determine whether a person is "loyal to the cause" and a "team player."

As you surely know, litmus is a dye obtained from certain lichens that is red under acid conditions and blue under alkaline conditions. So...if you live in the U.S., are you from a "red state" or a "blue state"?

If you live somewhere else, are you a member of the Red Team (conservative) or the Blue Team (liberal)? Be careful of your choice. Be sure about what jersey you put on, because no deviation

> We are just one conversation from paradise.

is permitted in this kind of deeply divisive politics. Individual thinking by members of a group or party is not allowed.

Of *course* I would like humanity to seriously consider the ideas here, and maybe even adopt a few of them, but I believe that the simple proposing of the ideas should be enough.

If they have true merit, the benefit of adopting and embracing them will be self-apparent. If not, the ideas should be dismissed.

Now I could be wrong about many of the concepts and approaches that I'm going to suggest here for inclusion in our New Cultural Story. People may read these and stamp them REJECTED. The choice is always theirs. But I'm hoping they'll at least *explore* the thoughts presented here. That exploration alone, that single, civil conversation, can affect a great deal.

I said it before and I'll say it again. I believe that we are just one conversation from paradise.

I want paradise for you. I want you to know peace and joy in your life. I wish that for all of us. For your children and for mine. And for our children's children. One of my own children's children—granddaughter Clementine—was born on the very day that I'm writing this. So my yearning for this future has taken on a very poignant energy for me today.

Will you join me in the quest to create paradise for Clementine... and for *her* children's children...and for yours?

PART TWO

*Ring out the Old,
Ring in the New*

Mind-bending thoughts as
our co-authorship begins

THE INCREDIBLE STORY
WE'RE DEALING WITH NOW

OKAY, SO NOW WE'RE going to get down to it.

We're going to look now, right here, at the Old Cultural Story of humanity that I keep harping about. The story that's been creating all the problems.

I touched on this ever so briefly at the very outset of our time together here. I said that I just wanted to look at it quickly and then get to solutions fast. But now I want to expand on what I said then, as I promised that I would do. Because now we know what many of our solutions can be...we've talked about conversation as a tool for change, we've talked about focusing those conversations on the Seven Simple Questions...but we must, must, *must* be very clear *what the holdup has been*, so that we can finally break the logjam.

The wrong medicine for the wrong illness

The situation we find ourselves in as we move more deeply into the 21st century is that we are coming up with the wrong medicine for the wrong illness. What we think is wrong with us is not wrong with us, so what we hope is the solution is not the solution.

The biggest difficulty in the world today is that we continue trying to solve our problems at every level except the level at which the problems exist.

We first try to solve our problems as if they were political problems, because we are used to using political pressure on this planet to get people to do what they don't want to do.

We hold discussions, we write laws, we pass legislation and adopt resolutions in every local, national, regional, and global language and assembly we can think of to try to solve the problem with words—*but it does not work*. Whatever short-term solutions we may create evaporate very quickly, and the problems reemerge. They will not go away.

> The biggest difficulty in the world today is that we continue trying to solve our problems at every level except the level at which the problems exist.

So we say, "Okay, these are not political problems and they cannot be solved with political means. They are economic problems." And because we are used to using economic power on this planet to get people to do what they don't want to do, we then try to solve the problems as if they were economic problems.

We throw money at them, or withhold money *from* them (as in the form of sanctions), seeking to solve the problems with cash. *But it does not work*. Whatever short-term solutions we may create evaporate very quickly, the problems reemerge. They will not go away.

And so we say, "Okay, these are not economic problems, and they cannot be solved by economic means. They must be military problems." And because we are used to using military might on this planet to get people to do what they don't want to do, we then try to solve the problems as if they were military problems.

We throw bullets at them and drop bombs on them, seeking to solve the problems with weapons. *But it does not work*. Whatever short-term solutions we may create evaporate very quickly, and the problems reemerge. They will not go away. And so, having run out of solutions, we declare: "These are not easy problems. No one expected that they could be fixed overnight. This is going to be a long, hard slog. Many lives will be lost in trying to solve these problems. *But we are not going to give up. We are going to solve these problems if it kills us.*" And we don't even see the irony in our own statements.

After a while, however, even primitive beings of very little consciousness become tired of the killing and the dying of their own sons and daughters in battle and their own women and children and elderly in the line of fire. And so, after enough killing has been done with no solution in sight, they say it is time to call a truce and *hold peace talks.* And the cycle begins again…

We are back to the bargaining table, and back to politicking as a solution. And peace talks often include discussion of reparations and economic recovery. And so, we are back to money as a solution. And when these solutions fail to work in the long run, we are back to bombs again.

And on and on and on it goes, and on and on and on it has gone throughout human history. Only the names of the players have changed, but the game has not.

Only primitive cultures and primitive beings do this. I know that you have all heard the definition of insanity. *Insanity is doing the same thing over and over again, expecting to get a different result.*

We can't seem to change our ways, however, because we are very used to trying to *force* solutions in our world.

Yet solutions that are forced are never solutions at all. They are simply postponements.

The great tragedy and the great sadness of humanity is that we are forever willing to settle for postponements in place of solutions.

Only primitive cultures and primitive beings do that. Highly evolved beings would never, *ever* settle for a *ten-thousand-year postponement* in solving their biggest problems. Here on this planet we've never really faced the largest problem of humanity head on. We refuse to. We pretend we don't even know what it is. And so we do our endless dance all around it. And we continue, century after century, to solve the world's problem *at every level except the level at which the problem exists.*

> The problem in the world today is a *spiritual* problem. It has to do with what people *believe.*

That is what I meant when I said at the very top of this conversation that *things are not what they seem.*

The problem in the world today is a *spiritual* problem. It has to do with what people *believe.*

It has to do with what they hold to be true about Life, about God, about themselves and about each other.

This problem of beliefs creates a condition of hopelessness, helplessness, anger, and rebellion. That condition produces a circumstance—*inevitably* produces a circumstance—of run-away violence.

The problem of beliefs is a problem which all of us have helped to create. This is true because all of us have beliefs. And all of us pass on those beliefs to others—to our children and our grandchildren and our neighbors and our friends.

We join together to create a Cultural Story…and *that Cultural Story is what creates the Conditions which produce the Circumstances that we are trying to eliminate and to avoid.*

Yet we cannot eliminate them and we cannot avoid them until we eliminate and avoid *the beliefs that created them*—and this is something we have staunchly refused to do. I don't think we even know what half of those beliefs are anymore.

Well, I'm going to fix that right now.

Here's what we're up against on this planet

Here is humanity's Old Cultural Story…as passed on to us by our parents, our teachers, our clergy, our political leaders, and everyone else whom we've counted on to know the truth. They told us…

We are born into a hostile world, run by a God who has things He wants us to do and things He wants us not to do, and will punish us with everlasting torture if we don't get the two right.

Our first experience in life is separation from our mother, the source of our life. This sets the tone and creates the context for our entire reality, which we experience to be one of separation from the Source of *all* life.

We are not only separate from all life, but from everything else *in* life. Everything that exists, exists separate from us, and we are separate from everything else that exists. We do not want it this way, but this is the way it is. We wish it were otherwise, and, indeed, we strive for it to be otherwise.

We seek to experience Oneness again with all things, and especially with each other. We may not know why, exactly, yet it seems almost instinctual. It feels like the natural thing to do. The only problem is, there does not seem to be enough of The Other to satisfy us. No matter what the Other Thing is that we want, we cannot seem to get enough of it.

We cannot get enough love, we cannot get enough time, we cannot get enough money, we cannot get enough of whatever it is we think we need in order to be happy and fulfilled. The moment we think that we have enough, we decide that we want more.

Since there is 'not enough' of whatever it is we think we need to be happy, we must 'do stuff' to get as much as we can get. Things are required of us to get everything, from God's love to the natural bounty of life. Simply 'being alive' is not enough. Therefore WE, like all of life, *are not enough.*

Because just 'being' isn't sufficient, there's stuff that we have to do. The ones who do the 'right stuff' get to have the things that they need to be happy. If you don't do the right stuff in the right way, you don't get to 'win.' Thus, the competition begins. There's 'not enough' out there, and so, we have to compete for it.

We have to compete for everything, *including God.*

This competition is tough. This is about our very survival. In this contest, only the fittest survive. Only to the victor go the spoils. If you are a loser, you live a hell on Earth, and after you die, if you are a loser in the competition for God, you experience hell again—this time forever.

Death was actually created by God because our forebears made the wrong choices. In Western theologies, the Myth of Adam and Eve tells us about this.

According to the myth, humans had everlasting life in the Garden of Eden, but then Eve ate the fruit of the tree of the Knowledge of Good and Evil, and she and Adam were driven from the garden by an angry God, who sentenced them, *and all their progeny forevermore,* to death as The First Punishment. Henceforth, life in the body would be limited, and no longer everlasting, and so would the *stuff* of life.

Many other cultures have their own Origination Stories, and most tell the same tale: one of Separation from God for one reason or another, and thus, the loss of everlasting life.

Yet God will give us back our everlasting life if we never again break His rules. God's love is unconditional, it is only God's rewards which are not. God loves us even as He condemns us to everlasting damnation. It hurts Him more than it hurts us, because He really wants us to return home, but He can't do anything about it if we misbehave. The choice is ours.

The trick is, therefore, to not misbehave. We need to live a good life. We must strive to do so. In order to do so, we have to know the truth about God's desire and what He does not want from us. We cannot please God, we cannot avoid offending Him, if we do not know Right from Wrong. So we have to know the Truth about that.

The Truth is simple to understand and easy to know. All we have to do is listen to the prophets, the teachers, the sages, and the Source and Founder of our religion. If there is more than one religion, and therefore, more than one Source and Founder, then we have to make sure to pick the Right One. Picking the Wrong One could result in us being a Loser.

When we pick the Right One, we are superior, we are better than our peers, because we have The Truth on our side. This state of being 'Better' allows us to claim most of the other prizes in the contest without actually contesting them.

We get to declare ourselves the Winner in the competition *before the competition begins.* It is out of this awareness that we give ourselves all the advantages, and write the Rules of Life in such a way that certain others find it nearly impossible to win the really big prizes.

> We are as a magician who has forgotten his own tricks.

We do not do this out of meanness, but simply in order to ensure that our victory is guaranteed—as rightly it should be, since it is those of our religion, of our nationality, of our race, of our gender, of our political persuasion, who know The Truth, and therefore deserve to be Winners.

Because we deserve to win, we have a right to threaten others, to fight with them, and to kill them if necessary, in order to produce this result.

There may be another way to live, another thing that God has in mind, another, larger Truth, but if there is, we don't know it. In fact, it is not clear whether we are even *supposed* to know it.

It is possible that we are not supposed to even try to know it, much less to truly know and understand God. To try is to be presumptuous, and to declare that you have actually done so is to blaspheme.

God is the Unknown Knower, the Umoved Mover, the Great Unseen. Therefore, we cannot know the truth *that we are required to know* in order to meet the conditions *that we are required to meet* in order to receive the love *that we are required to receive* in order to avoid the condemnation *that we are seeking to avoid* in order to have the everlasting life *that we had before any of this started.*

Our ignorance is unfortunate, but should not be problematical. All we need do is take what we think we DO know—our Cultural Story—on faith, and proceed accordingly.

This we have tried to do, each according to his or her own beliefs, out of which we have produced the life that we are now living, and the reality on Earth that we are creating.

Now you understand

Okay? That's it. That is how most of the human race has it constructed. We each have our variations, but this is, in essence, how we live our lives, justify our choices, and rationalize our outcomes.

And all this made-up stuff did not come out of thin air. It grew out of some very powerful *illusions* that appear to have been embraced by our species in the earliest days of its cognition. Or, using an analogy I like to employ, we are as a magician who has forgotten his own tricks.

All of this has created a world in which its richest countries in 2003 spent $60 billion to help the poorest countries address the problems of poverty, lack of education, and poor health, while during the same period spending *$900 billion* for defense.

Let me repeat that. Sixty billion dollars to help alleviate global poverty, nine *hundred* billion for defense.

This led the president of the World Bank to dryly suggest that if the world *simply reversed its priorities*, the cost of defense would never have to exceed the smaller sum.

I bring this up here not because I think that the solution to the world's problem is economic. (I have just made the point that it is not.) I bring this up because I believe that if we solved our spiritual problem, we would not *need* a huge budget for defense.

We would quite naturally shift our priorities into spending those defense funds to lift the poor out of the abject misery and hopelessness that produces the frustration and rage that the world now has to defend itself against.

People who aren't suffering do not attack others.

Yet the sign of a social order that is *really* failing is when even among those people in the world whose lives are more comfortable, violence is on an upswing.

If even those who should be *contented* are discontented, *you know something's wrong,* you know that something is fundamentally askew in the way you've got things set up. In short, you know you're in trouble. Big trouble.

All attack is a call for help. That's what *A Course in Miracles* declares, and I agree. If one person attacks another, it's because that first person is suffering. Violence is on an upswing not only on the streets of the Middle East, but on the streets of Europe; not only in the homes of the poor in Southeast Asia, but in the homes of the rich in North America, because of *poverty.* It is poverty that causes suffering.

> If one person attacks another, it's because that first person is suffering.

Poverty comes in many forms. There's financial poverty, physical poverty, mental poverty, or spiritual poverty…but it is all *poverty.* The human experience of need is widespread, and not exclusive to the poor. To put this another way, you could say that *the human experience of limitation is not limited.*

Need—perceived and unmet *need*—is what causes violence. And need is not solved by economic or political mechanisms. Need is a spiritual ill, solved by spiritual means.

Put in the spiritual solution, and need is seen for the illusion that it is.

Example: You would not let a member of your family die of starvation, standing right at your front door. Yet we allow 400 children an hour to die of starvation on a planet where there is more than enough to feed them. The problem is, we don't think of them as members of our family.

That's a spiritual problem, plain and simple. *We don't know Who We Are.* If we did, we would solve not only the needs of the poor at our front door, but also the affluent already seated at the table, but still striving for Bigger, Better, More.

POINTS I HOPE YOU WILL REMEMBER...

- Our Old Cultural Story is unworkable in these days and times. It was probably always unworkable, but the more spiritually aware and spiritually sophisticated we become as a species, the more we realize how unworkable it is.

- Our ideas about how life is are based in simple, correctable spiritual misunderstandings.

ACTION I HOPE YOU WILL TAKE...

- Share our Old Cultural Story with as many people as possible. Copy it or type it out, duplicate it and hand it out at your Seven Questions Discussion Group. Ask the group's members for comments on the story. Are there any parts of it that they, or you, catch yourself still living?

- Lead a discussion, write letters to editors, bring to group consciousness the present state of affairs in our world in which the globe's richest nations spend $60 billion annually to alleviate the conditions that create abject poverty and misery on our planet and that thus lead to seething frustration, anger, and, ultimately, violence against the rich—then spend $900 billion to defend themselves against that anger.

WHEN THE FIRST DOMINO
FALLS, THE REST WILL FOLLOW

I AM SURE THAT you can see from that one look at our Cultural Story why our world is in the shape it's in. I am sure you can see that this Story is neither beneficial nor sustainable.

This, then, is why I propose a global movement to *change* our Cultural Story; to explore it line-by-line and to rewrite it where we believe it serves us to do so.

But now, please understand. I'm not proposing a global *conference*, or a global *convention*, or a global *congress*, which would meet and propose such changes. We've already tried those approaches and they have not worked.

The League of Nations did not prove effective. Neither has the United Nations brought an end to the oppression of the masses, the killing of thousands, the suffering of millions. A new Worldwide Congress of Humanity would do no better.

The problems of humanity reside in the one place where most leagues and congresses and senates and legislatures and conferences and political conventions refuse to go: the Realm of Spirituality.

> Well, they shouldn't go there. There should be a sepa-
> ration of Church and State. Religion should have nothing
> to do with politics, and vice versa.

What should really have nothing to do with politics is *economics.* That's where the danger is. These two should never be allowed to mix.

There should be a law that says that all political decisions made in the halls of legislatures and congresses and senates may not be based on, or take into account, any economic considerations whatsoever, but be foundationed in one thing and one thing only: what is best for the largest number of people.

There should be another law that bars any contributions of any kind to political candidates or parties by any economic interests (in other words, companies or corporations) or any firm representing any economic interests.

There should be a third law that simply says that corporations are not *persons*, and shall not be accorded rights equal to those accorded to people. (This law alone would solve much!)

Everyone in the United States is so intense about maintaining a separation between Church and State when the real concern should be about keeping a separation between Corporations and State—because in America (and most of the rest of the Western World, for that matter) *economics is the real religion.*

> What should really have nothing to do with politics is *economics.* That's where the danger is.

People believe that their personal life is threatened at the most basic level if political decisions are made that appear to impinge in even the slightest way upon their economic choices—*even when those political decisions are demonstrably for their own good,* such as basic government regulation of the health-care system; or government moves to guarantee safety in certain manufacturing fields; or regulations that protect consumers in certain food processing, storage, and shipping industries, to use a few simple examples.

Anything that regulates the business community and the economic system is seen as limiting basic America *freedom*—yet when that economic system *itself* limits people's choices (such as virtually monopolizing particular areas of commerce—airlines and computer software companies, among others, come to mind—locking out all competition, then setting the rules of the game and refusing to create compatibility between their products and those of others so that people must make a *forced buy* to get what they want in the so-called Free Marketplace)....when the economic system does *that*, this is called the Free Enterprise System, and we don't care *how* much we are abused by it. This is real *freedom!*

The economy was meant to be a way for members of a community— including the global community—to help each other ("You do this for me and I'll do this for you and we'll share the wealth that comes from sharing our individual gifts"), but it has turned out to be a way that people in the world get hurt. Most people. The majority of people.

> Believe it or not, the economy was never meant to control our lives.

A tiny minority of people are served and enriched by the economy, but the majority of people are enslaved and subjugated by it.

Believe it or not, the economy and economics was never meant to control our lives, but control them it does. Even (and perhaps most especially) our political system is tyrannized by it and beholden to it, and so the control of commerce over community is complete. We've allowed it to be—and *that*, as much if not more than the mixing of Church and State, is the real threat to our freedom.

But I digress. I want to talk more about this in the latter part of this conversation, which deals with specific ideas that could fit into our future Cultural Story. For now, getting to your question directly, I want to say that you are right, religion should have nothing to do with politics, just as you say. But...spirituality *should.*

Remove one, but not the other

The *Conversations with God* dialogue offers quite a bit of commentary about separation of Church and State. It may indeed be decided in some countries that Church and State must be separate, *CWG* notes. Based on results, people may determine that religion and politics do not mix. But, says this remarkable dialogue, *spirituality* is another matter.

Do not imagine that spirituality and politics do not mix, *CWG* says. Politics *are* spirituality, *demonstrated*. Political decisions represent—or at least are *supposed* to represent—the highest values held by people. And if if the living out of our highest values is not what spirituality is all about, then what *is* it about…?

Conversations with God goes on to observe: "The reason you may decide that Church and State should be separate is that Church means a very specific theological point of view, a particular religious belief. You may have observed that when such particular and specific beliefs inform your politics, you create great controversy, resulting in political strife."

> Spirituality is Life, and all that Life is.

I have seen this in America on issues such as gay marriage, abortion, and even something as purely scientific and obviously beneficial to humanity as stem-cell research. Elsewhere on the planet religion has produced equally contemptuous intrusions into the lives of people—the religious and the nonreligious—through its mixture with politics.

On the very day of writing this paragraph, I happened to read on the Internet that the people of Malta had just then voted to permit divorce in their country. Now there is only one country left in the world, the Philippines, in which divorce is *against the law.* Not against the law of a church, against the Law of the Land.

The referendum on Malta passed with just over 53% of the population approving. In other words, *it almost failed.*

How in the world did such a law exist for so long in this country? Four words: the Roman Catholic Church. News reports said that at mass in Catholic churches all over Malta on the day of the referendum, a letter was read to all congregants from the Archbishop of Valletta stating that people should vote "no" in the referendum.

Such religious pressure was a significant part of the "No" campaign, news reports said, with posters all over the island reading: "Jesus Yes, Divorce No."

Under the same influence of religion in politics, Ireland only passed its own law legalizing divorce in 1995. There, the move required *an amendment to the constitution.*

And so it is easy to see how divisiveness—sometimes bitter, vitriolic divisiveness—results when political and *religious* views mix like this, for the simple and obvious reason that not all people hold the same religious beliefs. Indeed, some people hold no religious beliefs at all.

But we are not talking here about religion. We're talking about spirituality. The experience of spirituality, *Conversations with God* says, is universal. Every human being on the planet has felt, at one time or another, a natural impulse for knowing of, and reunion with, the Divine.

Some have talked themselves out of it. Others have moved even more fully into it. Not a single person has never felt it. For this thing called "spirituality" is the call of Life Itself. It is Life, calling *to* Life, to experience and create *more* Life. That impulse resides in every living thing.

Says *Conversations with God*: "All people participate in it, even if they do not know it, even if they do not call it that. This is because 'spirituality' is nothing more than Life Itself."

One's spirituality is about one's deepest personal understandings of, and interactions with, Life and God, whatever those may be. They may be mystical and they may be practical. A person's experience does not have to be mystical to be spiritual.

Spirituality is not about a particular group's teachings and doctrines. It is about the values, ethics, and deepest experience of the individual, not the theological dogma of the clump.

The most basic tenet of spirituality is that All Things Are Part of Life. How can anything that appears *in* Life (physical and nonphysical, including understandings, beliefs, and behaviors) not be *part* of Life?

"You can argue all you want about whether there is a God, and whether all things are part of God, but you cannot argue about whether there is Life, or whether all things are part of Life," the *CWG* dialogue wryly observes.

Spirituality is, therefore, Life, and all that Life is.

"The only discussion then left is whether Life and God are the same things. And," the dialogue informs us, "they are."

The dialogue says that even an agnostic—even an atheist—would agree that there's some force in the Universe that is holding it all together. There is also something that *started* it all. And if there's something that started it all, there must have been something existing before the Universe as you now know it existed.

The Universe didn't just burst into being out of thin air. And even if it did, "thin air" is *something*. Yet even if you say that the Universe burst into being out of Nothing at All, still you must deal with the question of First Cause. What *caused* Something to arise out of Nothing at All?

In my conversation with God, I was told that this First Cause was Life Itself, expressing in physical (that is, visible) form. Some people call this the Big Bang. Whatever you call it, it was *life*, exploding into physicality.

"No one can disagree with this, because this is obviously 'what's so.' You can, however, argue forever (and you have!) over how to describe this Process; what to call it," says *CWG*, which does not equivocate. "This is God," it says. "This is what you mean, what you have always meant, by the word 'God.' God is First Cause. Unmoved Mover. That Which Was before That Which IS...The Alpha and the Omega. The Beginning and the End."

Connecting the dots

If spirituality is really another word for life, then that which is spiritual is Life Affirming, because *life* is Life Affirming.

Remember when I said that life is nothing but energy; that it is pure energy that circles back into itself? I observed then that life is a self-fueling, self-sustaining, self-determining, and self-creating process. It *depends* on itself, *relies* on itself, *looks* to itself to *tell* itself what the next expression of itself shall be. In other words, life is Life Affirming.

This is true universally, it is true globally, it is true nationally, it is true locally, and it is true individually. It is merely a matter of proportion.

And so we see the Universe deciding about itself in this way, our planet deciding about itself in this way, our nation deciding about itself in this way, our own city or community deciding about itself in this way, and our own *person* deciding about itself in this way. We observe that Life *informs* Life *about* Life *through the process of Life Itself.*

To inject spirituality into our politics, therefore, would be to *make all political activities and all political decisions Life Affirming.* And indeed, is this not exactly what we are trying to do with our politics?

The only reason we created politics in the first place was to produce a system by which life could be lived harmoniously, freely, happily, and peacefully. In other words, a system by which life itself may be affirmed.

I must admit that I had never thought of it quite that way until I had my conversations with God, but then I saw that this is exactly why humanity created political systems, of course! In the United States the Founding Fathers even *said so*, explicitly. The U.S. constitution declares that all men are created equal, with certain inalienable rights, among them *life, liberty, and the pursuit of happiness.*

Most governments elsewhere were created for basically the same reason. There may be differences in the *form*, but never the *purpose*, of government. Different cultures and societies may spell out differently their ideas and goals and how to achieve them, but their fundamental desires are nearly identical.

We see, then, that spirituality and politics obviously mix, given that spirituality is about values, and so are politics. The latter is *based* on the former!

> Yet every time a country's government has been used
> to enforce a particular religious point of view, the result
> has been oppression of all those within that country who
> do not adopt that religious view. And often, by the way,
> *war* with people *outside* of that country.

I agree. I see this, too. I see some nations forcing religious doctrine into people's lives through draconian civil laws, resulting, for instance, in the flogging of women in public who are seen sitting in a public place next to men who are not husbands or blood relatives; or men having their shops closed because they have not grown a beard.

It is why most people in most nations around the world have told themselves that spirituality is the realm of the individual and should have nothing to do with collective governance—even though they want their collective governance to reflect the highest values of the individual. It's a Catch 22.

So creating a New Cultural Story that would simply replace old limiting beliefs and ancient ethno-specific behavioral rules with *revised* limiting beliefs and *new* draconian behavioral rules would do nothing to help the world.

What is needed is a brand new set of beliefs, utterly different from the old, and capable of being embraced by the whole of humanity, not only by certain religious groups.

POINTS I HOPE YOU WILL REMEMBER...

- Religion should be kept out of politics, but not spirituality.

- Life informs life about life through the process of life itself.

- Our New Cultural Story cannot simply replace old limiting beliefs and ancient ethno-specific behavioral rules with *revised* limiting beliefs and *new* draconian behavioral rules.

ACTION I HOPE YOU WILL TAKE...

- Write a letter to your legislators urging them to remove business and commerce from politics. Join a global *movement* to do so.

- Work in your community to inject more spiritual values into the political decisions being made there. Become politically active, rather than passive, so that it isn't others to whom these decisions are left, but you.

THE MORPHIC FIELD, THE TIPPING POINT, AND CRITICAL MASS

WHAT IS BEING INVITED here is a new human manifesto, a Declaration of Interdependence for the entire world. What our species is begging for is a New Cultural Story, a new way of understanding life, a new way of being human.

I do not see this new story, however, as some sort of Statement of Universal Understandings that will be proposed to our entire species at one moment for simultaneous adoption. That would simply be another Top Down Pronouncement from some Power Source—and who or what would that Power Source be?

Rather, I see this New Cultural Story as emerging from the only legitimate power source of any enlightened society: every member *of* that society. I see it as the product of cordial and collaborative interplay and interaction between people around the world through conversations about, and persuasive demonstrations of, the "wonderfulness" of the New Story itself.

I predict that the potential of this collaboratively created New Cultural Story to produce individual joy and group peace will become self-apparent, and that its adoption by a critical mass of people will become so desirable that this will occur almost automatically. I see this as the last great, and the gentlest, revolution.

Yes, that is a good name for it…

…The Gentlest Revolution.

I think you're living in a bubble. You imagine that people are going to adopt a New Cultural Story automatically?
People don't do that, man. They gotta be practically forced.

I'm not sure that's true. Most people usually don't have to be forced
to do what's in their own best interests if it is patently obvious that it *is*
in their own best interests.

Really? I know people who are aware that stopping
their smoking habit is in their own best interests, yet you
have to practically force them to do it.

I know people who are aware that eating less fat-
tening food is in their own best interests, yet you have to
practically force them to do it.

I know people who are aware that exercising is in their
own best interests, yet you have to practically force them
to do it.

I know people who—

—Okay, I'm going to agree with you in part. It's true that not *everyone* automatically does what's in their best interest. Maybe even not the
majority of people. But I believe that a *critical mass* will. And when the
first domino falls, the rest will follow.

That's a lot of people you're going to have to convince. "Critical mass" is a lot of people.

Actually, not as many as you might think. I'm told that "critical
mass" is not 51% of any whole, nor is it 25%, nor is it 10%, nor is it
even 5%. Critical mass in some cases can be achieved when something
between 2.5% and 3.5% of the whole is affected.

If you want to see this demonstrated, watch a pot of water come to a
boil. Half of its surface is not bubbling when the water reaches a boiling
point. Not even a quarter of its surface. Just watch the water. As it heats
up you'll see a bubble here and a bubble there…maybe three to four percent of the surface showing bubbles…then, *whammo!* The whole surface
breaks out. You've just witnessed critical mass.

So we're not talking about three or four billion people here. Or even one billion. Or even half a billion.

The wonderful online source *Wikipedia* tells us that "social factors influencing critical mass may involve the size, interrelatedness and level of communication in a society or one of its subcultures."

The reference also notes that "small changes in public consensus can bring about swift changes in political consensus."

We know that to be true. We know that a global undertaking such as The Conversations Movement can bring humanity to a tipping point.

We're confident that when sufficient numbers of people begin to contribute to the co-authoring of our New Story (and begin to talk about it), there will be a shift in the morphic field sufficient to produce global resonance around the observation that our Old Cultural Story is simply no longer working, and that the creation of a New Cultural Story is a very, *very* good idea.

> A global undertaking such as The Conversations Movement can bring humanity to a tipping point.

(It was Rupert Sheldrake, an English biochemist and plant physiologist, who first proposed such a thing as a "morphic field." His books and papers stem from his theory of morphic resonance and cover topics such as animal and plant development and behaviour, memory, telepathy, perception, and cognition in general.

His publications include *A New Science of Life* [1981], *Seven Experiments That Could Change the World* [1995], *Dogs That Know When Their Owners Are Coming Home* [1999], and *The Sense of Being Stared At* [2003]. [Source: http://en.wikipedia.org/wiki/Rupert_Sheldrake])

Sheldrake says that "morphic fields" bring about nonlocal effects in consciousness and learning. We're counting on that, exactly. We believe that The Conversations Movement can and will produce just such exponentially expanding nonlocal effects—or what I have called "critical mass."

> You think so? I'm not so sure. I still think you're underestimating the stubbornness of people to change.

Not where their own best interest is concerned. We can achieve critical mass here. People driving around the traffic circle at the Arc de

Triomphe in Paris—where there are no lane markings, no traffic lights, no signs showing who goes first or where, and no police officer to direct the endless flow of cars—do not have to be forced by any law or regulation to yield the right-of-way, or to stop before smashing into others, or to go when others have stopped. They do so *automatically.*

That's different. You're talking about survival there.

We're talking about survival *here.*

Let me show you something really interesting. Globally syndicated social commentator Thomas L. Friedman wrote in an op-ed piece on June 7, 2011 titled "The Earth is Full." Read this. It's very clear—and it explains exactly what I'm talking about here…

THE EARTH IS FULL

by Thomas Friedman

You really do have to wonder whether a few years from now we'll look back at the first decade of the 21st century—when food prices spiked, energy prices soared, world population surged, tornados plowed through cities, floods and droughts set records, populations were displaced and governments were threatened by the confluence of it all—and ask ourselves: What were we thinking? How did we not panic when the evidence was so obvious that we'd crossed some growth/climate/natural resource/population redlines all at once?

"The only answer can be denial," argues Paul Gilding, the veteran Australian environmentalist-entrepreneur, who described this moment in a new book called 'The Great Disruption: Why the Climate Crisis Will Bring On the End of Shopping and the Birth of a New World.'

"When you are surrounded by something so big that requires you to change everything about the way you think and see the world, then denial is the natural response. But the longer we wait, the bigger the response required."

Gilding cites the work of the Global Footprint Network, an alliance of scientists, which calculates how many "planet Earths" we need to sustain our current growth rates. G.F.N. measures how much land and water area we need to produce the resources we consume and absorb our waste, using prevailing technology. On the whole, says G.F.N., we are currently growing at a rate that is using up the Earth's resources far faster than they can be sustainably replenished, so we are eating into the future. Right now, global growth is using about 1.5 Earths. "Having only one planet makes this a rather significant problem," says Gilding.

This is not science fiction. This is what happens when our system of growth and the system of nature hit the wall at once. While in Yemen last year, I saw a tanker truck delivering water in the capital, Sana. Why? Because Sana could be the first big city in the world to run out of water, within a decade. That is what happens when one generation in one country lives at 150 percent of sustainable capacity.

"If you cut down more trees than you grow, you run out of trees," writes Gilding. "If you put additional nitrogen into a water system, you change the type and quantity of life that water can support. If you thicken the Earth's CO_2 blanket, the Earth gets warmer. If you do all these and many more things at once, you change the way the whole system of planet Earth behaves, with social, economic, and life support impacts. This is not speculation; this is high school science."

It is also current affairs. "In China's thousands of years of civilization, the conflict between humankind and nature has never been as serious as it is today," China's environment minister, Zhou Shengxian, said recently. "The depletion, deterioration and exhaustion of resources and the worsening ecological environment have become bottlenecks and grave impediments to the nation's economic and social development." What China's minister is telling us, says Gilding, is that "the Earth is full. We are now using so many resources and putting out so much waste into the Earth that we have reached some kind of limit, given current technologies. The economy is going to have to get smaller in terms of physical impact."

We will not change systems, though, without a crisis. But don't worry, we're getting there.

We're currently caught in two loops: One is that more population growth and more global warming together are pushing up food prices; rising food prices cause political instability in the Middle East, which leads to higher oil prices, which leads to higher food prices, which leads to more instability. At the same time, improved productivity means fewer people are needed in every factory to produce more stuff. So if we want to have more jobs, we need more factories. More factories making more stuff make more global warming, and that is where the two loops meet.

But Gilding is actually an eco-optimist. As the impact of the imminent Great Disruption hits us, he says, "our response will be proportionally dramatic, mobilizing as we do in war. We will change at a scale and speed we can barely imagine today, completely transforming our economy, including our energy and transport industries, in just a few short decades."

We will realize, he predicts, that the consumer-driven growth model is broken and we have to move to a more happiness-driven growth model, based on people working less and owning less. "How many people," Gilding asks, "lie on their death bed and say, 'I wish I had worked harder or built more shareholder value,' and how many say, 'I wish I had gone to more ball-games, read more books to my kids, taken more walks?'

To do that, you need a growth model based on giving people more time to enjoy life, but with less stuff."

Sounds utopian? Gilding insists he is a realist.

"We are heading for a crisis-driven choice," he says. "We either allow collapse to overtake us or develop a new sustainable economic model. We will choose the latter. We may be slow, but we're not stupid."

(A version of this op-ed appeared in print on June 8, 2011, on page A23 of The New York Times under the headline: The Earth Is Full.)

You see? It is like those drivers circling the Arc de Triomphe. They may be slow, but they are not stupid.

POINTS I HOPE YOU WILL REMEMBER…

- Our species is begging for a new way of being human.

- The potential of a collaboratively created New Cultural Story to produce individual joy and group peace will become self-apparent.

- A global undertaking such as The Conversations Movement can bring humanity to a tipping point.

- People are not stupid. They will not allow collapse to overtake humanity.

ACTION I HOPE YOU WILL TAKE...

• Help create critical mass around a new story for humanity. Join The Conversations Movement by going to *www.TheGlobalConversation.com*

• Help to write the New Cultural Story, then help to spread it.

A BRAND NEW STORY
FOR A BRAND NEW DAY

NOW WE'RE GETTING TO IT! Here comes the fun part! Here's where the conversation starts moving in exciting new directions.

Let's begin exploring ideas for a New Cultural Story by taking a look at what that old story we read about in Conversation 16, only with a little different twist, yes?

We'll use that old story as a template, simply *overwriting* new ideas on top of it. A good portion of my thoughts about humanity's New Cultural Story have come from the *CWG* dialogues. So I'm reaching into the many messages that I had shared with the world in lectures and in workshops and in my writing for many years, placing before us once again some ideas that I have always believed could change our world.

(Not everyone, of course, has heard my lectures or read my books, so for them these expressions will be brand new. If you're one of those who has heard some of this from me before, I'm hoping that this reminder of what our lives *could* be like will be even more enticing the second time around.)

So here, following, is the parallel of the Old Cultural Story that was outlined in Conversation #16. It might be interesting for you to bookmark both places, then bounce back and forth between them, comparing the old story to this new one....

"We are born into a friendly world, created by a God who has nothing that He wants us to do and nothing that She wants us not to do, and who will never punish us for anything at all, because our new understanding of God will make it clear that God is unable to be hurt or damaged, disappointed or angered in any way.

"Our first experience in physical life is of Oneness with our mother, the source of our life, as we experience it in the womb. This sets the tone and creates the context for our entire reality, which we experience as Oneness with the Source of *all* life.

"We are not only One with All Life, but with everything else *in* life. Everything that exists, exists in unity with us, and we are One with everything else that exists. We are so happy that it is this way, because this offers us a direct experience of the most significant aspect of Ourselves. We are glad it is not otherwise, and, indeed, we strive to make sure that no one imagines for even a moment that it *is* otherwise, and that they are alone.

"We seek, in the living of our lives, to express Oneness with all things, and especially with each other. We know and understand why, exactly, that it seems almost instinctual, that it feels like the natural thing to do. It is because Oneness is our natural state, and it is instinctual for us to express our natural state of being.

"There is no problem even if, in a moment of confusion, there does not seem to be enough of any Other person, place, or thing to satisfy us, because by returning to our Core Value and our Deepest Truth we know that the source of everything we could possibly desire lies within us—for the precise reason that God and we are One.

"We therefore experience ourselves as always having enough of everything. We always have enough love, always have enough time, always have enough money, and always have enough of whatever it is we think we need in order to be happy and fulfilled. The moment we imagine, in a temporary confusion, that we do not have enough, we return to our Core Value and our Deepest Truth and we see the illusion.

"Since we are clear that there is 'enough' of whatever it is we think we need to be happy, we realize that we don't have to 'do stuff' to get as much as we can get. We know that nothing is required of us to get everything, from God's love to the natural bounty of life. Simply 'being alive' is enough. Therefore WE, like all the things in life, *are enough*.

"Because just 'being' is sufficient, and there's no 'stuff that we have to do,' life is not a process by which the ones who do the 'right stuff' get to have the things that they need to be happy.

"*Everyone* gets to have those things…and the so-called right stuff doesn't exist anyway, since there is no such thing as 'right' and 'wrong.' Because you don't need to do the right stuff in the right way, you don't 'win' or 'lose' in life, you simply live it joyously, always. Thus, *no competition* with anyone else *is necessary.* There's 'enough' out there, and so we don't have to compete for it.

"We don't have to compete for anything, *especially God.*

"Life is not a competition that is tough, and our experience and purpose is not about survival, it is about expression. Specifically, the expression of Divinity in, through, and as Us, and the experience of heaven on earth.

"There is no such thing as 'only the fittest survive,' or 'to the victor go the spoils.' You cannot be a loser, and so you get to live a heaven on Earth. And after you die, you cannot be a loser in the competition for God, either, for there is no such competition. Thus, you will experience heaven again—this time forever.

"What we call 'death' was created by God as part of the process of evolution. It is not the end of our existence, however, but rather, a simple transformation from one life form into another, as is birth. Both are part of the everlasting and eternal journey of the soul from the Realm of the Spiritual to the Realm of the Physical and back again.

"The Western theological myth of Adam and Eve is an Origination Story created by humans who did not understand and could not explain death, and so created a tale which was both totally inaccurate and completely unbelievable. Nevertheless, many people embraced the allegory, until humanity's New Cultural Story was at last written in the first quarter of the 21st century.

> We don't have to compete for anything, *especially God.*

"Many other cultures around the world had their own Origination Stories, and most told the same tale: one of Separation from God for one reason or another, and thus, the loss of everlasting life. But now those cultures, too, have abandoned their Old Story in favor of the New Cultural Story of Humanity.

"The New Story tells us that God never took away our everlasting life, and that we don't have to worry about breaking His rules, because She doesn't have any. God's love is unconditional, and so are God's rewards.

"God loves us and would never condemn us to everlasting damnation, even if there were such a thing, which there is not. God has made it possible for all of us to return Home, and nothing can stop that process—even if we do what we call 'misbehave.'

"There is no such thing as 'misbehaving' in the mind of God, any more than you would say that an innocent baby has misbehaved. We are the children of God, and God sees us in exactly this way. The New Cultural Story tells us: 'If you saw you as God sees you, you would smile a lot.'

"The trick is, therefore, to not imagine that we can misbehave. We were designed to live a good life, and it is only our misguided thought about who we are and how life is that can interrupt this process. We must strive to stop mistaken thinking. For it is as Shakespeare wrote: 'Nothing is evil, lest thinking make it so.'

"In order to set aside mistaken thinking, we have to know the truth about God's desire and what God does and does not want from us. We have to know that God wants nothing at all, because God *has* and *is* Everything. What, then, could God possibly want or need from us?

"We do not, therefore, have to worry about pleasing God, we do not have to seek to avoid offending Her or angering Him. We merely have to know that there is no such thing as Right and Wrong, only that which serves, that which Works or Does Not Work, depending upon what it is we are trying to do. We have to understand the Truth about that.

> It is not to our benefit to give ourselves all the advantages.

"The Truth is simple to understand and easy to know. All we have to do is listen to the prophets, the teachers, the sages, and the Source and Founder of our religion. Not to those who have subsequently misinterpreted them, but to the Sources and Founders themselves.

"There is more than one religion, and therefore, more than one Source and Founder, but they all spoke the same basic truth. Because this is so, there is no way to pick the Wrong One. All religions speak truth at their core. It is the misinterpretation of their messages, and the 'add-on' messages, that have rendered so many of their current teachings inaccurate and misleading.

"Because all religions, at their core, speak truth, there is no way to pick the 'right one' and thus declare yourselves to be superior, or better than your peers, because you have The Truth on your side.

"It is now clear to everyone that this state of being 'better' is an illusion, which in the past allowed some people to falsely claim most of the prizes in what they imagined to be the contest of life. They declared themselves to be the Winner in a competition, ignoring the fact that competition was not needed.

"The New Story has made it clear to everyone that it is not to our benefit to give ourselves all the advantages, and to write the Rules of Life in such a way that certain others find it nearly impossible to win the really big prizes. And so, no one does this anymore.

"Because humans do not do this anymore, peace and joy is guaranteed—as rightly it should be, since no matter what our religion, our nationality, our race, our gender, or our political persuasion, we deserve to be winners in life. God has set it up to be a process with no losers.

"Because we all deserve to win and we all *do* win, we have no need or desire to threaten others, to fight with them, or to kill them in order to produce this result.

"There is no better way to live than to live without competition, without insufficiency, without the requirement to mollify an angry and vindictive God, without need of any kind, and with only love as our constant expression and experience. To live this way is to live as if we were Divine, and that is exactly how God designed life to be lived. There is no other thing that God has in mind, no other, larger Truth, and so there is no need to search for one.

"Everything there is to know about Life we are *supposed* to know, and the knowing of it is very easy. All we have to do is live inside the truth of love. All we have to ask is, What would love want? What would love do? What would love give? With these simple questions it is possible to truly know and understand God.

"God is not the Unknown Knower, but the Knower that resides within all of us, the Unmoved Mover, the Great Unseen. Therefore, we can easily know the truth of Who We Are and Who God Is. All we need to do is go deeply inside, to the Source of our Everlasting Knowing, and ask God to reveal Itself there.

"True ignorance is impossible, and is one of the Ten Illusions of Humans. All we need do is embrace what we now know—our New Cultural Story—and live its basic message of love. If we seek to do this, each according to his or her own ability, we will produce the life for which we have all yearned, and the reality on Earth of which we have long dreamed."

Just a start, just a beginning

I know it's a long narrative, but hang on, because right now I'm going to break this down into groupings, each with identical categories, so that we can take a look at how all the broad-based concepts above would function in every day beliefs and every day life—*after* we look at how they are functioning for most human beings *now*.

We've been talking here about co-creating, with you, a New Cultural Story that could change *beliefs*. That is the core here; that's the shift that must occur if we are to create a new humanity, a new way of living, a new reality; if we are to complete the Overhaul of Humanity in a way that brings an end to The Storm Before the Calm and moves us into the Calm itself.

I'm going to say it again. *We have to change our beliefs.*

About what?

About a lot of things…and most important, about God. And let me tell you why.

Much of our lives is wrapped up in what humanity believes about God, and about what God expects and demands and requires of us. This is true because our cultures, our customs, or morals, our social mores, our business ethics, and our codes of conduct are all *built* around our understandings of God.

This is not surprising in a world where the vast majority of people in every corner of the world profess a belief in some sort of Power Greater (by whatever name or description).

But it is not only our cultures, customs, morals, mores, ethics and codes that are wrapped up in our concepts of God and God's commands. Much of our *civil law* from country to country is based on religious doctrines. And religious doctrines, of course, are based on human interpretations of what are considered Divine Demands.

I went to *Wikipedia* not long ago and looked up the origin of laws. I learned that the Roman Catholic Church has the oldest continuously functioning legal system in Western Europe, predating the common and European civil law traditions. I discovered that what began with rules ("canons") adopted by the Apostles at the Council of Jerusalem in the 1st century has blossomed into a highly complex and original legal system encapsulating not just norms of the New Testament, but some elements of the Hebrew (Old Testament), Roman, Visigothic, Saxon, and Celtic legal traditions spanning thousands of years of human experience.

You can find out this same stuff by following this link...

http://en.wikipedia.org/wiki/Canon_law

...but let me save you the trouble. The encyclopedia tells us that the institutions and practices of canon law paralleled the legal development of much of Europe, and that "consequently both modern civil law and common law bear the influences of canon law."

Wikipedia informs us that Edson Luiz Sampel, a Brazilian expert in canon law, says that canon law is contained in the genesis of various institutes of civil law, such as the law in continental Europe and Latin American countries. Sampel explains that *canon law has significant influence in contemporary society.* (Italics mine.)

The most famous ancient civil code is the Corpus Juris Civilis, a codification of Roman law (remember that phrase) produced between 529—534 AD by the Byzantine emperor Justinian I, which forms the basis of civil law legal systems.

Other civil codes used since ancient times include various texts used in religious laws, such as the Law of Manu in Hindu law, the Mishnah in Jewish Halakha law, the Canons of the Apostles in Christian Canon law, and the Qur'an and Sunnah in Islamic Sharia law to some extent.

Historically, "Roman law" also denotes the legal system applied in most of Western Europe, until the end of the 18th century. In Germany, Roman law practice remained longer, having been the Holy Roman Empire (963–1816); thus the great influence upon the civil law systems in Europe.

Moreover, the English and North American Common law also were influenced by Roman law. And Roman civil law that applied only to Roman citizens *was bonded to religion.* (Italics mine again.)

I've gone into this in some detail here because I want you to know that I wasn't kidding when I said that what humanity believes about God, and about God's expectations and requirements of us, affects every person—even those who themselves do not believe in God at all.

Not the least of the ways in which we are all affected has to do with beliefs held by millions about what God has set down for human beings as acceptable behavior. I'm talking about human society's basic ideas about "right" and "wrong."

Let's take a look at what many of us have been taught about that, shall we? This is going to be very instructive. Eye-opening, actually.

POINTS I HOPE YOU WILL REMEMBER...

- We were born into a friendly world.

- We are not only One with All Life, but with everything else *in* life.

- God would never condemn us to everlasting damnation.

- Everything there is to know about Life we are *supposed* to know, and the knowing of it is very easy.

- What we believe about God and about God's desire and demands is important even to agnostics or atheists, because our civil laws throughout the world are based in more than small measure on religious doctrines.

ACTION I HOPE YOU WILL TAKE...

- Write your own version of a New Cultural Story for humanity.

- Post your new story on the website at *www. TheGlobalConversation.com*

- Make a list of the laws where you live that you see are clearly based on religious doctrines or beliefs (Laws against gay marriage, for instance? Or forbidding stem-cell research?) and begin a campaign, working with others, to repeal those laws.

CAN YOU BELIEVE
WHAT WE BELIEVE?

HERE IS A QUICK survey of some of the things many people have been told by their ancestors, by their parents, by their teachers, and by other authority figures in their lives about *God's desire*. It may be tough for some of you to get through this survey. Please do it anyway.

Let's take the most obvious topics first.

Regarding *God*…many humans have been told that God's desire is for humans to understand that God is the Supreme Being, the Creator of Heaven and Earth, the Giver of Life, Omnipotent, Omniscient, Omnipresent, and Wise Beyond Human Understanding.

God is the Alpha and the Omega, the beginning and the end, the Unmoved Mover, separate from humanity, but the creator of it in His own image. Separate from life, but the Creator of it, as His gift to humanity.

Most humans have been told that God is a single God, a unified God, the Only God there is. The word *Allah* means, literally, *the God*. Some humans have been told that this One God is divided into Three Parts, one of which became human. Some humans have been told that there is more than one God. And some humans have been told that there is no God at all. The majority of humans in the 21st century believe in a God of some sort.

Most of those who do believe in God have been told that *God's desire* is Love and Justice.

To fulfill the first mandate, God has granted each human being ample and repeated opportunity to be reconciled with Him.

To fulfill the second mandate, God, at the end of each human life, sits in Judgment of every human soul, deciding at this Reckoning whether the soul has earned everlasting reward in Heaven or everlasting damnation in Hell.

Most humans have been told that God is a jealous God, God is a vengeful God, God is an angry God who can be filled with wrath and who uses violence directly on human beings—and who invites and even commands human beings to do so on each other.

They've also been told that God is a caring God, a compassionate God, a merciful God, a loving God who wants nothing but the best for human beings. All that humans have to do is obey Him.

It's easy for humans to know how to obey God because God has told humans exactly what to do and what not to do. It's all there in Sacred Scripture. It can be found also in the words and in the teaching of God's personal representative on Earth.

These are the beliefs of much of humanity.

One result of this teaching: Many human beings are afraid of God. They also love God. So, many humans confuse fear and love, seeing them as connected in some way. Where God is concerned, we love to be afraid (we have made it a *virtue* to be "God fearing"), and we are afraid not to love (we are commanded to *"Love the Lord thy God with all thy mind, all thy heart, and all thy soul"*).

Humans fear what God will do to them if they do not obey Him. They have been told He will punish them with everlasting torment. Many human beings therefore rely heavily on their understanding of God's word and God's desires and what meets God's approval when regulating their lives, interpreting situations or events, and making decisions.

When U.S. President George W. Bush was asked if he ever sought the advice of his father, the first President Bush, he replied that he sought counsel from "a higher Father." When the then new spiritual leader of Hamas, Abdel Aziz Rantisi, delivered a speech at Gaza's Islamic University in March 2004, he told those assembled that "God declared war" against America, Bush, and Israeli Prime Minister Ariel Sharon. Rantisi added, "The war of God continues against them and I can see the victory coming up from the land of Palestine by the hand of Hamas." Two weeks later Rantisi was dead, killed by an Israeli rocket attack on his car.

Earlier it was said, "Humanity's ideas about God produce humanity's ideas about life and about people."

This is painfully clear. This is painfully obvious.

———— ·◆· ————

Regarding God's word and God's messenger...many humans have been told that God's desire is for God's Word to be recognized as being contained in the Holy Scriptures and Sacred Texts, and for God's Messenger to be honored and listened to and followed.

There are many Holy Scriptures and Sacred Texts, including the Adi Granth, the Bhagavad-gita, the Book of Mormon, the Hadith, the I Ching, the Kojiki, the Lun-yü, the Mahabharata, the Mathnawi, the New Testament, the Pali Canon, the Qur'an, the Tao-te Ching, the Talmud, the Torah, the Upanishad, the Veda, and the Yoga-sutras, to name a few. Many humans have been told that only one of these texts is the right one. The rest are wrong. If you choose the teachings of the "wrong" one, you'll go to hell.

There are many Messengers, including Noah, Abraham, Moses, Confucius, Siddartha Gautama (who has been called The Buddha), Jesus of Nazareth (who has been called The Savior), Muhammad (who has been called The Greatest Prophet), Patanjali (who has been called The Enlightened One), Baha'u'llah (who has been called

> Many human beings are afraid of God.

the Blessed One), Jalal al-Din Rumi (who has been called the Mystic), Paramahansa Yogananda (who has been called the Master), Joseph Smith (who has been called many things), and others. Many humans have been told that only one of these messengers is the right one. The rest are wrong. If you choose the message of the "wrong" one, you'll go to hell.

One result of this teaching: Human beings have been trying to figure out which is the right text and who is the right messenger for thousands of years. The followers of certain messengers and the believers in certain texts have sought to convince the rest of the world that the messenger and text of their persuasion is the only one to which people should turn.

On many occasions throughout history, these attempts at conversion have turned violent. There has scarcely been a day on this planet when a battle has not been fought or a human being not killed in the name of God, or for God's Cause.

The Holy Scriptures of all major religions indicate that vanquishing, punishing, and killing is something that God Himself has repeatedly done; and so vanquishing, punishing, and killing in God's name and in the name of God's Messenger is acceptable and, in some circumstances, required.

This is, many of the world's people believe, God's desire.

Regarding heaven and hell...many humans have been told that God's desire is for people to live good lives, and for good people to go to Heaven or Paradise after their deaths; while bad people go to Hell, Gehenna, or Hades. Those in Heaven will live in unending bliss in reunion with God, and those in Hell will live with other evildoers who have been damned to eternal torture. Where each individual soul goes will be decided at the Reckoning on Judgment Day.

Some humans have been told that hell is a temporary experience during which sinners are tormented by demons until the debt created by the evil of their lives has been paid, while others have been informed that hell is but a phase in a soul's journey as it passes through many experiences of reincarnation.

One result of this teaching: Millions of people have structured their entire lives around the struggle to avoid "going to hell" and around the hope of "getting to heaven." They have done extraordinary and sometimes shocking things to produce this outcome.

The concept of heaven and hell has shaped not only their behavior, but their entire understanding of life itself. It has also shaped human history.

Regarding life...many humans have been told that God's desire is for life to be a school, a place of learning, a time of testing, a brief and precious opportunity to migrate the soul back to heaven, back to God, whence it came.

Many humans have also been told that it's when life ends that the real joy begins. All of life should be considered a prelude, a forerunner, a platform upon which is built the soul's experience of eternity. Life should therefore be led with an eye toward the Afterlife, for what is earned now will be experienced forever.

Most humans also believe that *God's desire* is for people to understand that life consists of what people can see, hear, taste, touch, and smell—and nothing more.

One result of this teaching: Humans believe that life is not easy, nor is it supposed to be. It's a constant struggle. In this struggle, anything other than what is perceived by the five senses is considered "supernatural" or "occult" and falls, therefore, into the category of "trafficking with the Devil" and "the work of Satan."

Humans are struggling to get back to God, and into God's good graces. They are struggling to get back home. This is what life is about. It's about the struggle of the soul, living within the body, to get back home, to return to God, from Whom it has been separated.

Most people of religious persuasion focus heavily on Heaven and Hell. Those who believe that "getting to Heaven" is the ultimate Purpose of Life, and who truly and fervently believe that they can *guarantee* their entrance into Heaven by doing certain things while on Earth, will, of course, seek to do those things.

They'll make sure that their sins are confessed regularly, and that their absolutions are up to date, so that if they die suddenly their soul will be ready for Judgment Day. They'll fast for hours, days, or weeks at a time, travel on pilgrimages to distant holy places, go to church or temple or mosque or synagogue every week without fail, tithe 10% of their income, eat or not eat

> Humans believe that life is not easy, nor is it supposed to be.

certain foods, wear or not wear certain clothing, say or not say certain words, and engage in all manner of rites and rituals.

They'll obey the rules of their religion, honor the customs of their faith, and follow the instructions of their spiritual leaders in order to demonstrate to God that they are worthy, so that a place will be reserved for them in Paradise.

If they are distressed enough and oppressed enough and unhappy enough, some humans will even end their own lives and kill other people—including the totally innocent and the absolutely unsuspecting—for the promise of a reward in heaven.

(If that promised reward happens to be 72 black-eyed virgins with whom to spend all of eternity, and if the humans in question happen to be 18- to 30-year-old men with little future and a dust-laden, poverty stricken, injustice-filled present, the chances of their making such an extraordinarily destructive decision will increase tenfold.)

They'll do this because they believe this is God's desire.

But is it?

———— •——•————

Regarding gender…many humans have been told that God's desire is for humanity to understand that God is male. The result is that most people who believe in a deity at all hold this to be true. The idea that God is masculine is so pervasive that it's shocking to the ear to hear God referred to as "She."

Many humans have also been told that God wants men and women to have particular roles and to be treated in particular ways in life, and that He has specified all of this in Holy Scripture.

One result of this teaching: Males are considered superior to females in nearly all of the world's cultures. In some of those cultures, this manifests as cultural norms that do not allow females to go to school, to hold jobs of authority or responsibility, to leave the home without being in the company of a blood male relative, or to permit any part of their body to be seen in public, requiring them to be covered from head to toe.

A woman's testimony at Court is worth half of that of a man's—meaning that it requires two female witnesses to meet the test of adequate proof. A woman's testimony regarding a husband's beatings, cruelty, or infidelity will go ignored unless she can produce a corroborating witness, whereas a man can send his wife to death by stoning by simply stating that she committed adultery. His singular assertion is sufficient.

A woman's share of any inheritance is also accepted as being half of that of her brother. The logic behind this is that a man is financially responsible for his family, while a woman is not.

This is the identical logic that, in other cultures, blocks women from earning the same pay as men for doing the same work. The fact that a man may remain unmarried all his life and wind up not having a family, or that many women become widows, or that women would not and should not *have* to concede this role to a man if she were treated equally, is, of course, ignored by this logic.

In some male-dominant cultures, female's genitals are mutilated, cut and sewn, in order to deprive them of sexual pleasure and thus reduce the temptation they may feel to engage in sexual encounters other than those demanded by their husbands. In some cases this is seen as a rite of passage rendering female children desirable, suitable, and worthy marriage material.

Other cultural norms reflecting extreme bias against females include the custom of blocking women from becoming clergy in many religions or rising to power and authority in any civil, legal, or business enterprise, or holding any major leadership position in politics or government.

A handful of women in some cultures have overcome these customs (in many cultures they are still not allowed to even try), but always it's a struggle, always it's the notable exception, always it's a steep uphill climb to be accepted in most high-profile occupations or powerful or influential roles within the global society.

This difference in the treatment of the genders is, many of the world's people believe, God's desire. After all, the Bible says so. And so do the Scriptures of other religions.

Regarding marriage…many humans have been told that God's desire is for marriage to be an everlasting union between a man and a woman, for better or for worse, for the purpose of propagating the species and maintaining a civil society organized into family units, which supports God's agenda for humanity.

One result of this teaching: In most religious cultures, ending a marriage for whatever reason, including mental or physical cruelty, is deeply discouraged; and one major religion tells its followers that they may never divorce, may never remarry in the church nor receive the church's sacraments if they do divorce, and may never marry another person who has been divorced.

In many places and cultures, marriage rules are established by religion, then become civil law, limiting and constricting the behavior of marriage partners—and those limits remain in place for life. Chief among those limits is what humans call "fidelity." Human beings living in marriage must remain faithful to each other. That is, they may not have sexual experiences with anyone else for the rest of their lives—not as a matter of personal devotion or sacred agreement, but as a matter of civil law.

> The idea of male supremacy, drawn from the concept of God as male, has a major effect in many marriage scenarios.

This should not be surprising since, as has just been noted, prohibitions against many kinds of private sexual activity have been placed in the common culture by religions. According to their accounts of *God's desire,* human beings may not have sex with anyone outside of marriage, with anyone prior to marriage, and, therefore, should they never marry, *at no time during their entire lives.*

This is the expectation, and humans are told that the breaking of this taboo can lead to severe punishment, from God and from the social environment.

As a result, marriage is entered into by many young people around the world who are neither ready for such a commitment nor sufficiently mature for the responsibilities attached to it, but who are unwilling to endure any longer the prohibition against sexual experience.

The idea of male supremacy, drawn from the concept of God as male, has a major effect on many marriage scenarios. In some cultures marriage is considered a form of ownership and servitude, with the woman being the owned object—actually *paid for* with a dowry—and the male being the person served. Even in cultures with less extreme views, a wife is expected to be "obedient" to her husband, and to be subservient to him in every way. The man is "the head of the household."

This is, many people believe, God's desire.

Regarding sex and sexuality…many humans have been told that God's desire is for sexual union to be experienced only with one's spouse for the purposes of procreation and the expression of love.

One result of this teaching: Millions of people believe that sex may absolutely never be experienced in any way that deliberately prevents conception; and that while sex is wonderful, to experience sex simply for pleasure with no possibility of procreation is against the will of God and, therefore, "unnatural," immoral, shameful, and a giving in to baser instincts.

As with the combining of fear and love in the earlier understanding of God, the combining of pleasure and shame in this construction has produced chronic emotional confusion: wonder, excitement, and passion; yet embarrassment, fear, and guilt about sexual desires and experiences.

In most cultures the sexual parts of human bodies may not be referred to by name. The words *vagina* and *penis* are not to be used in public (except as absolutely necessary in a purely clinical setting), and never with small children. The words *wee-wee, pee-pee,* or *bottom* may be used freely. In short, the human culture agrees that the actual names of certain body parts are shameful and embarrassing and are to be avoided whenever possible.

Again, you may believe that the above assertion is a bit of an exaggeration. I assure you it is not. Internationally known columnist Molly Ivins reported in the September/October 2004 issue of *Mother Jones* magazine that Advocates for Youth, a group working for comprehensive sex education, had its funding for AIDS prevention yanked by the Center for Disease Control, a U.S. government agency, because "young people [in the project's video] used the correct terminology for male and female anatomy."

That, said James Wagoner, head of Advocates for Youth, "is absurd. What is the president going to do? Issue an executive order that every man, woman, and child should refer to the penis as a dingaling?"

And, of course, if one cannot *speak* of certain body parts, one certainly cannot *show* them. Not even, apparently, to oneself. Yet another exaggeration? I'm sorry to say, no. So puritanical is the viewpoint on all of this in many places that the following letter could actually appear, without anyone blinking an eye, in over 300 newspapers in the United States on September 25, 2004, in an advice column:

Dear Abby:

I went to wake up my 14-year-old daughter today and discovered her sleeping in the nude. Apparently she has been doing it for some time.

Normally she is good about getting up and I haven't needed to enter her room to awaken her. When I asked her why she does it, she said it's more comfortable and she sleeps better.

When I told her I was not comfortable with it, she asked me why, and frankly I could not come up with a good reason other than it seemed "wrong," and fear about what would happen in an earthquake or fire. She questioned how it could be wrong if no one knows—unless they walk into her room without knocking (as I did).

She keeps a long robe next to the bed so she can put it on in case of emergency. (Indeed, she walks around the house in that robe, and I thought she had a night-gown underneath, when in fact she has been naked underneath since Christmas.)

I am still not comfortable with it, but we agreed to abide by your advice. Is it OK for her to sleep in the nude, and why—or why not?
—*Worried Mom in San Leandro*

The columnist wrote back that there was "nothing inherently wrong" with sleeping in the nude. "Look at the bright side," she advised the mother. "It makes for less laundry."

As this parent's letter makes clear, many humans feel that certain body parts must be covered and hidden, having been deemed too arous-ing or too shameful, or both. For those parts not to be covered is incor-rect and unacceptable. Indeed, in many places it's actually *illegal*, with punishments in *civil law* for those who fail to obey.

Many people believe that sex experienced in certain ways, even between husband and wife, is "unnatural" and therefore immoral. And again, in many times and places, some experiences, although between consenting adults, have actually been made *illegal*. Those who wrote such legislation said that they understand that God does not want certain sexual experiences to occur. God sends people to hell for this.

> Millions of humans believe that sexual energy and spiritual energy do not mix.

Humans also believe that intensely graphic depictions of sexual activity in photographs, drawings, comic books, video games, television and motion pictures are distasteful, repugnant, disgusting, and unacceptable. Intensely graphic depictions of extreme physical violence and killing are, however, entirely acceptable.

Millions of humans believe that sexual energy and spiritual energy do not mix. They have been told that sexual energy is a "lower chakra" energy, and that sexual activity and spiritual clarity essentially oppose each other. Persons seeking to achieve spiritual mastery are therefore advised against engaging in sexual experiences. Some are actually required to remain abstinent.

This is, many of the world's people believe, God's desire.

Regarding homosexuality...many humans have been told that God's desire is for sex to be experienced between a male and a female only, and for same-gender sexual interaction to be considered an abomination.

One result of this teaching: Humans for whom same-gender sexual attraction feels most natural have been denounced, vilified, condemned, ostracized, isolated, assaulted, and killed by people who believe they are doing God's will.

The sad account of the killing of Matthew Shepard in Laramie, Wyoming, offers us a now-famous case in point. Shepard, an openly gay freshman at the University of Wyoming, was dragged out of a bar in Laramie by two young men, driven to a deserted road outside of town, tied to a cow fence, and beaten so severely that he lapsed into a coma and died five days later.

His youthful assailants were apprehended and sentenced to life in prison, but the Reverend Fred Phelps, pastor of the Westboro Baptist Church of Topeka, Kansas, was not inclined to let the matter rest there. Every year for the five years following Matthew's brutal beating and death, this Christian minister has traveled to Laramie, as well as to Casper, Wyoming, Matthew's birth place, to "celebrate" his death.

And, according to a report in the *Los Angeles Times* by reporter David Kelly, on October 12, 2003, Reverend Phelps brought with him to Casper a granite monument engraved with Matthew's face, followed by these words chiseled in stone:

"Matthew Shepard Entered Hell October 12, 1998 at age 21 In Defiance of God's Warning: 'Thou shalt not lie with mankind as with womankind; it is abomination.' Leviticus 18:32."

It was the Reverend Phelps who also attended Matthew Shepard's funeral and, as the young man's parents, family, and friends stood in mourning, screamed: "God hates fags!"

With this level of clarity as to the Divine Intention and Desire, entire countries have been forced under power of governmental authority and rule of law to obey God's Will in this matter.

In some nations the civil penalty for homosexuality is death—burial under a 12-foot concrete wall. In many places civil law has been created making gay marriage illegal. In the United States the president in 2004 personally campaigned to have his understanding of God's desires regarding prohibition of gay marriage written into his country's Constitution.

> Many people are very confused about the true nature of love.

While certain sexual feelings may be very natural to the persons feeling them, they are not God's desire, many people say, and are therefore, by definition, "unnatural." A report on October 20, 2003, by Chris Zdeb of CanWest News Service in the *Calgary Herald* in Edmonton, Canada, points to the possibility that the exact opposite may be true.

"Scientists have discovered 54 genes that suggest sexual identity is hard-wired into the brain before birth, and before development of the sex organs," the journalist reports, and goes on to say:

"The findings released today by a team of University of California, Los Angeles, researchers could mean that sexuality, including homosexuality and transgender sexuality, are not a choice."

Nevertheless, the clergy of many of the world's largest religious denominations continue to assert that God condemns such sexual experiences.

"I didn't write the Bible," Archbishop Peter Akinola of Nigeria has been quoted in the press as saying. "It's part of our Christian heritage. It tells us what to do. If the word of God says homosexuality is an abomination, then so be it."

There you have it. And this gentleman does not stand alone, but echoes what many members of the clergy tell their congregations, declaring that the afterlife consequence of engaging in homosexual activity is everlasting damnation and torture in the fires of hell.

This is, those people believe, God's desire.

Regarding love…many humans have been told that God's desire is for love to be conditional. God has made it clear that He loves humans if they do what He wants. If they do not, humans shall know His wrath. They'll be condemned to everlasting damnation.

Some say that God acts with love when He condemns people to eternal and unending torture. With this explanation they seek to preserve the image and the notion of a loving God.

One result of this teaching: Many people are very confused about the true nature of love. Human beings "get," at some deeply intuitive level, that the imposing of unending punishment is not a loving thing to do. Yet they are told that such punishment is a demonstration of the purest and highest love. It's God's love in action.

It's not unusual for human beings to therefore be afraid of love, even as they have been made afraid of God, who is the source of love. They have been taught that God's love can turn into wrath in a flicker, producing horrifying results.

This packaging of love and fear in human theology has not been without consequences in human behavior.

Earlier it was said, "Humanity's ideas about God produce humanity's ideas about life and about people." This is profoundly true, and thus, many humans are afraid of, and attracted to, love at the same time.

Often their first thought upon moving into a closer love relationship with another is, "Now what is this person going to want, or need, or expect from me?" That is, after all, the nature of their love relationship with an all-powerful God, and they have no reason to believe it will be any different with a much weaker human being.

There is also the corollary thought that partners in a relationship have a *right* to expect certain things in exchange for love—that love is a give-and-take, *quid pro quo* proposition.

These expectations and fears undermine many love relationships at the outset.

Because love and the worst torture imaginable have been linked in the minds of humans as natural activities on the part of God, most humans believe that it's right and proper to punish other humans for their behaviors—just as God does.

In perhaps the most dramatic demonstration of this, many human beings believe that it's appropriate to kill human beings as a warning to human beings that it's inappropriate to kill human beings.

This is, many of the world's people believe, God's desire.

Regarding money…many humans have been told that God's desire is for money to be considered the root of all evil. Money is bad and God is good, and so money and God do not mix.

One result of this teaching: The higher one's purpose and the greater one's value to society, the lower one's income must be. Nurses, teachers, public-safety officials, and those in similar service professions are not to ask to make much money. Ministers, rabbis, and priests are to ask even less. Homemakers and mothers, under this guideline, should have no personal income at all. If they want something for themselves, they may ask their husband for a few dollars, or scrimp pennies from the grocery money.

The message here is: Because "filthy lucre" is bad, because money is intrinsically evil, pay must be in reverse proportion to the value of the function performed. The better the deed, the worse the pay. People should not get lots of money for doing good things. And if they're doing something really, really, *really* good, they should want to do it for free.

Humans have created a disconnect between "doing good" and being well compensated. On the other hand, doing things of somewhat less lasting intrinsic value can produce compensation in the millions. So can illegal activity of all kinds. Thus, society's values discourage noble actions and encourage triviality and illegality. Humanity's watchword is: the higher the purpose, the lower the reward.

This is, many of the world's people believe, God's desire.

Now for a bit of the abstract

How are you doing here? I know this is taking a while, but that's because, as I said, the influence of the teachings we have all received about God runs deep. It embraces philosophical areas as well as the practical aspects of life.

Even though the following final topics touch upon concepts that we may think we'll encounter only in the abstract, the fact is that how we think about these abstractions affects—and *creates*—our concrete moment-to-moment experience.

Regarding free will…many humans have been told that God's desire is for human beings to have Free Will. Thus, they may determine and decide for themselves which of the Ultimate Outcomes—heaven or hell—they wish to experience after their death. They may do as they choose at any moment, at every juncture. They are not restricted in any way.

Humans have been told that God has granted humanity this Free Will so that humans may freely choose God, freely choose God's Way, and freely choose to be reunited with God in heaven. In other words, they may freely choose to be good, as opposed to being forced to do so. God wants humans to return to God by *choice*. No one should be required to do so.

Human beings have also been told that under the doctrine of Free Will, while people may do as they choose, if they do not choose *God's desire* they'll pay for it with continuous torture through all eternity. No element of duress is seen in this. It's simply the Way Things Are. It's Justice, at the highest level. It's God's Justice, which follows God's Judgment. It's important, therefore, to freely choose *God's desire*.

One result of this teaching: Humanity's concept of freedom has been deeply affected and profoundly shaped by its understanding of what God means by "freedom." Humans have decided that freedom doesn't have to mean *freedom,* but can mean simply the ability to select outcomes.

This is better than having no choice at all, and so humans in positions of power have learned to use the word "freedom" to privately describe the process by which they get others to do as they as are told.

People don't have to do as they are told, of course. But if they do not, there will be a price to pay. That could mean anything from having taxes audited to being thrown in jail for two years without charges being filed and without any explanation other than being labeled a threat to the security of the country. Using this measure, nations call themselves "free."

Most people, except, perhaps, the most stubborn apologists, see the contradiction in all of this. They understand perfectly well that no people are truly free who face the most horrendous outcomes imaginable if they don't do what they're told. Only a hypocrite or a fool would call such a choice "free."

Humans have learned, then, that hypocrisy—especially hypocrisy for the "right" purpose, in the "right" cause—is acceptable on Earth as it is in heaven. Much of humanity's political activity has been informed by this ethic. And elsewhere within the spectrum of human activity as well, in the way many humans communicate with each other, in the way many deal with each other, it has come to be understood that the end justifies the means.

In fact, many humans have now convinced themselves that none of this is hypocrisy at all. It's simply a matter of *interpretation.*

And so, in this day and age, freedoms are taken away in the name of Freedom itself. Millions of people gratefully embrace the political rhetoric that says *lack* of freedom is what guarantees their freedom, and the religious doctrine that says their choices in life are free only if they do as they are told, because this is God's desire.

Regarding suffering…many humans have been told that God's desire is for suffering to be used by human beings to better themselves, and to purify their soul. Suffering is good. It earns credits, or points, in God's mind, especially if it's endured silently, and maybe even "offered up" to God.

Suffering is a necessary part of human growth and learning and is, more important, a means by which people may be redeemed in the eyes of God.

Indeed, one whole religion is built on this belief, asserting that all beings have been saved by the suffering of one being, who died for the sins of the rest. This one being paid the "debt" said to be owed to God for humanity's weakness and wickedness.

According to this doctrine, God has been hurt by the weakness and wickedness of humanity and, in order to set things straight, *someone has to suffer.* Otherwise, God and humanity could not be reconciled. Thus, suffering was established as a redemptive experience.

With regard to the suffering of human beings due to "natural" causes, it's not to be shortened by death under any circumstances that are not also "natural." The suffering of animals may be mercifully ended

> Humans have decided that freedom doesn't have to mean *freedom,* but can mean simply the ability to select outcomes.

before "natural" death, but not the suffering of people. It's God and God alone who determines when human suffering shall end.

One result of this teaching: Human begins have endured unimaginable suffering over extended periods in order to do God's will and not incur God's wrath in the Afterlife. Millions of people feel that even if a person is very, very old and is suffering very, very much—lingering on the verge of death but not dying, experiencing interminable pain instead—that person must endure whatever life is bringing them.

Humanity has actually created civil law declaring that people have no right to end their own suffering, nor may they assist another in ending theirs. However anguishing it may be, however otherwise hopeless a life may have become, the suffering must go on.

This is God's desire.

Regarding morality…many humans have been told that God's desire is a moral society.

One result of this teaching: Humanity has spent its entire history attempting to define what is moral and what is not. The challenge has been to come up with a standard for society that does not change, all the while the society itself is changing.

To find this "gold standard," many societies have turned to God or Allah or Yahweh or Jehovah or whatever other name they have used to designate Deity, and have relied on their understanding of *God's desire*.

Many centuries ago, God's preferences in this matter were given a powerful label. They were called "natural." This is because the concept of a Deity first entered the minds of primitive humans as a result of their earliest observations of and contacts with Nature. Here was something bigger than they were, something they could not control, something they could only stand by and watch, hoping for the best.

> In most human societies it's not an individual's actual experience, but the society's *definition* of it, that determines its morality.

"Hoping for the best" soon transmuted into what would now be called praying. Whoever and whatever this Deity was, early humans reasoned, it was deeply connected with Nature, and Nature was an expression of It.

And so, humans created gods representing the sun, moon, and stars, the weather, crops, rivers, the land, and nearly everything else, in hopes of getting some control over things—or at least getting some communication going with whoever *did* have control.

From this connection of God and Nature it was only a short mental hop to consider that all things having to do with deities and gods were "natural," and all things not having anything to do with deities were "unnatural."

When human language came into form, the words "God" and "Nature" became inextricably linked. Certain conditions, circumstances, and behaviors were then described as "natural" or "unnatural," depending upon whether they adhered to or violated the current perception of the Will of God.

That which is "unnatural" has, in turn, come to be described as "immoral"—since it's not of God, and cannot, therefore, be *God's desire*. The circle thus completes itself. Anything that is not considered "natural" is considered "immoral." That includes all "unnatural" abilities, powers, behaviors—and even thoughts.

The idea that *God's desire* is what is natural, and that what is natural is what is moral, has not been a perfect measure, but it has been the best that humanity has been able to do in the search for an unchanging standard.

It's for this reason that humanity has been loath to change its ideas about God's desire. Changing those ideas changes the gold standard of human behavior.

Behavior is the currency of human interaction. Beliefs about God's desire gives value to the behavioral choices of humans, just as gold gives value to the pieces of paper called money.

Thus, in most human societies it's not an individual's actual experience, but the society's *definition* of it, that determines its morality. This is the case with homosexuality.

It's also the case with a great many other behaviors, such as prostitution, premarital sex, depictions of explicit sexual activity, the use of peyote, marijuana, and other plants and stimulants, or even the experience of ecstasy not induced by any outside stimulant.

For instance, if one says one has had an ecstatic experience of God, but if the experience does not fall within what humanity currently defines as "natural," it's considered immoral and to be warned against and, if it's continued, to be condemned, and, if it's still continued, to be punished.

In previous times it was often punishable by torture or death. More than one saint claiming and describing such ecstasies has been martyred in humanity's long history, using such guidelines.

Those saints were killed because the people killing them were convinced that they were doing God's desire.

Regarding death…many humans have been told that God's desire is for their wonderful life to eventually end, at which time their opportunity to learn and to grow is over and the time to be rewarded or punished for how they have lived begins.

One result of this teaching: Many humans consider that death is a terrible thing, and something to be feared. It's the End of the Line, the Final Curtain Call, the Closing Bell. Nearly all of the imageries surrounding death are negative, fearful, or sad—not positive, uplifting, or joyful. These imageries pervade our society. A street that goes nowhere is a Dead End. A person who is badly mistaken is Dead Wrong. The spirit who comes to retrieve your soul is The Grim Reaper.

Most people do not want to even talk about death, much less experience it. No one wants to experience it before he or she has to. People cling to life, sometimes desperately. The survival instinct is the strongest human instinct of all. Our common culture supports survival as the ultimate goal. Even people who *want* to die are not allowed to.

On the other side of death, many people feel certain, is the Final Judgment. If you have not been good, it's at this point that you'll go to hell. Your payment for all of your sins in this way is God's desire.

Humanity's list of God's desires is very long and covers many other areas of human experience not discussed here. As I've noted, that list forms the basis of innumerable civil laws, cultural traditions, social mores, and familial customs that touch all human beings.

So what do you think about what you've read here? With allowances for a few exceptions in wording here and there, or a slight difference in interpretation, is this basically what you remember being taught about what God desires, seeks, and requires from humanity?

Some of the ideas here first appeared in my book *What God Wants,* a publication that I had hoped might sponsor some changes. Alas, not much, if anything, has changed in the cultural story that many people have been continuing to tell their children around these topics since that time. This is part of what has made me very clear that for changes to occur—I mean, large-scale changes—more must happen than a single book being published. An entire global *conversation* must take place...and then, out of it, a worldwide movement. What is needed is The Gentlest Revolution. Hence, now, The Conversations Movement.

POINTS I HOPE YOU WILL REMEMBER...

- Separating God's desires into categories, we see with frightening clarity the stories we have created, and that billions of people continue to live by.

- Humanity's list of these desires and requirements of God is endless, yet in today's world very little of what we've placed on that list serves humanity.

ACTION I HOPE YOU WILL TAKE...

- Educate yourself. Go to a priest, a rabbi, an ulama, or a minister and ask for help in understanding their faith by going through the categories presented here and sharing with you their understanding of God's desire as it relates to the various topics on this list.

- Share this list with as many friends as you can, and ask them the same thing you asked the clergy. Find out what others around you believe about God's demands, desires, and declarations.

- Bring this list to your Seven Questions Discussion Group and go over it item by item, so that everyone in the group can know what human beings have been telling each other regarding these issues. It is important to understand the nature of the problem before seeking to solve it.

CAN YOU BELIEVE WHAT WE *COULD* BELIEVE, IF WE SIMPLY CHOSE TO?

I RECOGNIZE THAT IT took a bit of pluck, a bit of fortitude, to look closely at all of that. There's probably a bit of underbelly in there for all of us, some place where we feel particularly vulnerable. After all, a lot of this stuff was taught to us by some of the most venerable persons in our lives. Parents, grandparents, relatives, favorite teachers, the grey-haired soft-spoken priest, the wonderful and humorous minister, the wise and worldly rabbi . . .

But now the time for courage has *really* come. Now comes the part that some people of power don't want you to read, because they know you'll get all excited about it and that'll be the beginning of the end of their game. Now come some specific ideas that might form the basis for a first draft of humanity's new human story.

Chief among them is the idea that God and Life are One, that everything in life is part of a unified whole, and that our different belief systems are merely wonderfully divergent paths to the same destination—a destination the soul need not strain to reach, because it is already there: the everlasting embrace of God.

The doctrine of Oneness used as a basis for all human political, economic, social, educational, and religious decisions is the foundation of the New Cultural Story I am proposing.

Should we share this idea with enough people to create critical mass, should we succeed in shifting the resonant field, we can breathtakingly alter life as it is lived on Earth.

What kinds of changes might humanity see? What kinds of shifts could occur in your personal life? Back just a bit ago I offered you a narrative rollout of that. It was a broad, general narrative. Now have a category-by-category look at what I believe will happen. Here is one vision of what humanity's New Cultural Story could place into our day-to-day experience....

Regarding God...humans will understand that Allah, Brahmin, Elohim, God, Jehovah, Krishna, and Yahweh are among the many names humans have given to The One Thing That Is. They'll also understand that The One Thing That Is is all that exists. There is nothing that is not part of The One Thing That Is.

> Oneness used as a basis for all human decisions is the foundation of the New Cultural Story.

The Only Thing That Is is the Supreme Being, the Creator of Heaven and Earth, the Giver of Life, Omnipotent, Omniscient, Omnipresent, and Wise Beyond Human Understanding.

The Only Thing That Is is the Alpha and the Omega, the beginning and the end, the Unmoved Mover, not separate from humanity, but one with it, not separate from life, but one with it, both the Creator and the Created—with the Created necessarily then being in the image of The Only Thing That Is.

The Only Thing That Is wants and needs nothing. How could it? It's the only thing that is. It does not, therefore, sit in Judgment of anyone, nor decide at some sort of Reckoning whether a Part of Itself will be able to rejoin the Whole of Itself, since no Part was ever separated from the Whole, and could not be.

One result of this new teaching: No human beings will be afraid of God or Allah or Yahweh or whatever name they choose to give to The All In All. They'll simply love God completely and utterly as the amazing amalgam that God is.

Humans also will no longer confuse love and fear. They'll see clearly that these are mutually exclusive, that they cannot both exist at the same time in the same space. The effort to pretend that they can, that they somehow go together, is what has turned many humans into neurotic beings, trying to live out a reality that is completely out of alignment with what they instinctively know to be so, and completely contrary to their nature.

Regarding God's word and God's messenger...humans will understand that God's words are found in all of the world's Holy Scriptures, and that no scripture is more authoritative, more complete, more accurate, or more authentic than any other, but that each contains great wisdom and each leads to a greater understanding of The Only Truth There Is.

So, too, will humans understand that there are many messengers of The Only Truth There Is—indeed, that all people everywhere are messengers, and that their message is their life, lived. For life is a process by which life is informed about life through the expression of life itself. Life tells life about life through life. Humanity is what it shows itself to be. Every human being is both the Messenger and the Message.

One result of this new teaching: Human beings will stop trying to figure out which is the right text and which is the right messenger and will simply look closely to see which text and which messenger speaks to them in a way that makes it possible for them to understand the great mysteries and the great wonders of life. Humans will also stop trying to convince others that the messenger and the text that has touched their heart is the only one that people should turn to.

Wars and killing in the name of a particular text or messenger will be impossible to justify under these circumstances, and will all but disappear.

Heaven and Hell

Regarding heaven and hell...humans will understand that the Universe is not some outlying territory separate from Heaven, but that it's part of The Only Territory There Is. They'll come to understand that Heaven is the experience of traveling through that territory in a state of bliss—a state that may be reached at any time, no matter where within the territory of life one happens to be.

Humans will also understand that life is not a system of reward and punishment, and that no one is sent to hell or condemned by God.

At least one major world religious leader, Pope John Paul II, has already clarified this. He made a theologically breathtaking statement before a papal audience in Rome on July 28, 1999.

"Damnation cannot be attributed to an initiative of God because in His merciful love He cannot want anything but the salvation of the beings He created," the Pope declared to an astonished world. Eternal damnation is never the initiative of God, it's the self-imposed punishment of those who choose to refuse God's love and mercy, the pontiff added.

And what is this "damnation" that is referred to? Is it endless fiery torture in that place of flames called hell? No, said the Pope. Hell, he announced, does not exist as a place, but is "a situation in which one finds oneself after freely and definitively withdrawing from God, the source of life and joy."

> Life is not a system of reward and punishment, and no one is sent to hell or condemned by God.

The Pope said people must be very careful in interpreting the biblical descriptions of hell—the "inextinguishable fire" and "the burning oven"—which he said are symbolic and metaphorical. These picture phrases are meant to "indicate the complete frustration and vacuity of a life without God," John Paul said.

So what is the truth? Are any human beings in hell? That is, Pope John Paul II said, "not something we can know."

This is a remarkable statement from the spiritual leader of one of the largest religious organizations in the world. Asked that question ten years ago, there are very few priests, ministers, rabbis, or mullahs on the planet who would have responded with anything other than an immediate and unequivocal "Yes! What do you think we've been trying to tell you???"

But the Pope has apparently had some new ideas on this subject that are very much in concert with the New Cultural Story, because they eliminate the fear of hell as a theological tool with which to construct an entire spiritual reality that has deeply affected humanity.

One result of this new teaching: People's concept of life will no longer be shaped by a win-lose construction of the Afterlife. They'll begin to formulate new ideas of what is experienced after death. Humans will then no longer structure their lives around the hope of getting to heaven or the fear of going to hell.

They'll stop doing extraordinary, shocking, or self-destructive things to produce the first outcome. They'll find different reasons to act as they act, choose what they choose, say what they say, and think what they think. They'll create that new measure of morality for which the world has been searching.

Regarding life...humans will understand that life is not a school, neither is it a time of testing. If God wants nothing, there is no reason for a test. If humans are One with God, there is nothing to learn, there is only to remember what has been forgotten.

Humans will also understand that life is not an ordeal during which the soul struggles to get back to God, but rather, is an ongoing process by which the soul seeks to know God, then to grow, to expand, and to experience more of what it is. It will also be clear that this process, called *evolution*, never ends, but is experienced by the soul everlastingly, at different levels and in different life forms.

Humans will also understand that life is not limited to what can be perceived by the five senses, but is far wider in scope and deeper in dimension than humans at first imagined or have ever been told by religion.

One result of this teaching: Much more attention will be paid to what is not perceived by the five senses, and this will be the basis of a new understanding of life and how it might be most joyfully and wonderfully experienced.

Life will not be lived with an eye toward the Afterlife, but with an eye toward what is being created, expressed, and experienced at many levels of perception in the Holy Moment of Now. Humans will become increasingly aware that "now" is The Only Time There Is.

Life will not be experienced as a struggle or as an effort to "get back home" to God, but rather, as a free-flowing expression of one's intrinsic nature, which is unlimited and divine.

"Getting to heaven" will no longer be the ultimate purpose in life. *Creating* heaven wherever you are will be seen as the prime objective. To experience this, people will not have to confess any sins or fast during daylight hours or travel on pilgrimages or go to places of worship weekly or tithe regularly or perform any particular ritual or act—although they may choose to do any of these things if it pleases them, or helps to remind them of who they are in relationship to God, or assists them in staying connected with their purpose.

Because of their deeper understanding and rich personal experience of life as a unified field, for people everywhere life itself will become the prime value, and the core around which all spiritual understanding and expression revolves.

Regarding gender...humans will understand that God is not a male, nor is God a female, but that God has so gender at all.

Because the idea of God as a male being will be rejected as simplistic and inaccurate, humans will also understand that men are not superior to women in any way. The thought that God wants men and women to have limited roles in life will be abandoned in favor of a thought of complete equality for women and men. Indeed, with regard to all people everywhere, of whatever race, creed, gender, age, or sexual persuasion, the lack of superiority and the absolute equality of individuals will be The Only Thought There Is.

One result of this teaching: Discrimination and abuse of females will disappear from civil society.

Regarding marriage...humans will understand marriage to be a spiritual tool, a sacred device, used by evolving beings to play out their soul's agenda and to complete that part of their journey which involves mutuality with a particular Other for the purpose of growth and the continued recreation of Self.

They'll also understand that all human relationships are hallowed ground, that intimate relationships with a significant other are highly impactful and important, and that holy matrimony is a contract of extraordinary meaning and consequence.

Humans will be aware that no two souls meet by chance, but that every human encounter is purposeful and laden with gifts, and that every melding of hearts and partnership of souls, however long or brief, is the playing out of a mystical agreement—God's invitation to experience and expand in awareness, consciousness, understanding, and expression of the Divine Essence of Being.

One result of this teaching: People will not see marriage as an opportunity to complete themselves or to somehow bring to their lives "something that is missing," but to celebrate the fact that there is *nothing* missing, that they are Whole, Complete, and Perfect just as they are; and to expand and grow in their experience of this through the wondrous miracle of bonded relationship.

Humans will never again enter into or stay in marriages for reasons of security, because they'll understand that the only real security is not in owning or possessing, nor in being owned or possessed…not in demanding or expecting, and not even in hoping, that what they think they need in life will be supplied by another…but rather, in knowing that everything they desire in life…all the love, all the passion, all the wisdom, all the insight, all the power, all the knowledge, all the understanding, all the nurturing, all the compassion, and all the strength…resides within them.

Humans will see marriage as a truly Holy Communion, a union between two loving people lasting as long as both choose to be united, not a union that is required by God to be everlasting, for better or for worse. Humans will understand that the success of a marriage is measured by what has been given and received, understood and remembered, shared and healed, and by what growth has been produced.

And finally, all humans will understand that marriage is about teamwork, the teamwork of two souls who have created a holy team to do the holy work of life itself, which is the work of growth and the expression of divinity through the experience of unity. Those who have a truly holy union will know that their union is a *three-way union*, that their team consists of each other and of God, and that this is The Only Team There Is.

Regarding sex and sexuality…humans will understand that sexual union is a glorious and wonderful expression of the Oneness of Being, an extraordinarily powerful and deeply meaningful experience of the most intimate physical, emotional, psychological, and spiritual aspects of the self that two people can share; and a celebration of love and life that has no equal in physical form.

They'll also see clearly that sex is not laden with any taboos, do's or don't's, but is meant to be experienced joyfully by two consenting adults in whatever way brings pleasure and respects the boundaries, desires, and agreements of both.

Humans will also understand that the human body is sacred, not embarrassing; and that no part of the body is anything other than totally beautiful, and may therefore be shown and seen without shame.

One result of this teaching: Sexual guilt and sexual shame will virtually disappear from the human family. So will sexual assault. Sexual expression will be lifted to the level of the profound, never lowered to the level of the profane; and there will be no thought that spiritual energy and sexual energy do not mix, but rather, it will be taught that sexual energy is a beautiful expression of spiritual energy in physical form.

Many more people will become familiar with *tantric* sex, in which the sexual experience is expressed as sacred union. *Tantra* is defined as "the realization of the Oneness of the Self and the visible world," and when sex is experienced as sacred, it is, in physical form, The Only Tantra There Is.

Regarding homosexuality…humans will understand that there is no form and no manner in which the expression of a love that is pure and true is inappropriate.

One result of this teaching: Humans for whom same-gender sexual attraction feels most natural will no longer be denounced, vilified, condemned, ostracized, isolated, assaulted, and killed by people who believe they are doing God's will. Their wholesale discrimination and oppression will end.

Regarding love…humans will understand that love is neither quantifiable nor conditional. They'll know that the term "conditional love" is an oxymoron, and that love cannot be parceled out in units of varying size, but is either present or not present, in any given moment and with any given person, as an experience of the Whole Heart and Mind and Soul—a full expression of the Blessed Essence of Being Itself.

> No two souls meet by chance.

While humans will understand that love cannot be quantified, they'll see that it can be expressed in different ways, and that these different *kinds* of love are what they confused with different *levels* of love in the past.

Because it will be clear that God wants nothing from human beings and gives everything *to* human beings, God will be the ultimate model, at last, of what love is and means.

One result of this teaching: The veil of confusion around love will lift at last. Humans will use the term "love" to mean an entirely different thing than it now means in most human relationships. It will never again be confused or used interchangeably with the word "need."

The term "love" will be deeply respected, as it will be clear that it carries actual energy (as do all words, but this one to a very high degree) and produces more different and powerful vibrations than perhaps any other term in humanity's many languages, except the various names of Deity.

> There is no form and no manner in which the expression of a love that is pure and true is inappropriate.

Indeed, it will be very clear that there is no universal term, common to all languages, that comes closer to capturing the very Essence of God. Humans will see clearly that to define God in one word, "love" is The Only Term There Is.

Regarding money…humans will understand that money is simply energy, taking a particular form, and that, like any other energy, it has neutral value in and of itself.

They will also understand that "money" and "wealth" do not equal each other in absolute terms, and that true wealth has nothing at all to do with money.

Finally, humans will understand that God has nothing against money, and that the idea that money and spirituality do not mix is false.

One result of this teaching: Wealth will be redefined, with enormous consequences for society. What humans strive for, what humans work for, will have nothing to do with the accumulation of money, but, rather, the accumulation of *value* within their lives, for their families, and for humanity as a whole.

Money will be seen as being nothing more than a tool—one of many—that may be used in the creation of Mutual Value.

The redefining of wealth will also produce a new kind of currency. Equal Value Exchange Credits ("evecs") will be a new currency denomination, and it will take the form of any exchange, not merely the exchange of paper or coins or financial accounting credits, which brings equal value to both sides in a transaction.

Because the idea that money is "bad" and that money and spirituality do not mix will be dropped, humans will be freed of the feeling of guilt around having money, making it possible for persons who do good things for the world—even for those who do "God's work"—to earn more than modest amounts of money without being made wrong.

It will become clear that for society to become maximally functional, the highest honor might most beneficially be given to persons bringing to society what society itself says it values most.

Now, as before, a bit of the abstract

Again, let's explore some topics that may be a bit more abstract, but that are no less a part of the human experience. And let's see what the New Cultural Story will put into our reality, if the vision laid out in this conversation comes true....

Regarding free will...humans will understand that their will is truly *free*. They'll know that God will never cause them to suffer dire consequences in the Afterlife for making one choice over the other in life.

One result of this teaching: The contradictions will be taken out of God's promise to humans, and this will inspire humans to remove the contradictions from their own promises to each other. A new definition of "freedom" will be created, one that reflects what the word was always intended to mean—the complete and total lack of limitations of any kind.

Regarding suffering…humans will understand that God does not want anyone to suffer, ever, and certainly does not require any being to suffer needlessly or endlessly in order to "stay in good standing" with God, or do "what is right."

One result of this teaching: If they have any control over the circumstances, people will no longer require themselves or others to endure ongoing physical pain needlessly or endlessly. People will also understand the difference between suffering and pain, observing that pain is an objective experience, while suffering is a subjective decision about it.

Many mothers experience the pain of childbirth not as suffering at all, but as an intense but joyous celebration of life itself, *producing* life itself, through the *process* of life itself. Rising to this level of awareness about all pain is a matter of elevating one's consciousness and adopting a change of perspective, which can alter an entire experience. Thus, *Consciousness* is used as a transformative tool, creating in the human mind an experience of the body that defies exterior evidence—and transmutes it.

Regarding morality…humans will understand that morality is not unchanging, nor is it dictated by *God's desire*, since God wants nothing at all.

One result of this teaching: People will begin to take the question of defining morality firmly into their own hands, refusing to cede authority to any organization or institution. The outcome of this will be that contemporary morals will more authentically reflect contemporary behaviors. Humans will thus be able to act the way they have routinely acted, only doing so without guilt or fear of being judged, "outed," or condemned.

The argument that humanity's values will drop should this occur will not be validated, because people, given higher levels of responsibility for themselves, will be found to rise to higher levels of greatness in the creation and expression of who they are.

This is the purpose and the wonder of life, they'll see: *To constantly re-create myself anew in the next grandest version of the greatest vision ever I held about Who We Are—as a species, as individuals, and as divine beings in a causal universe.*

Regarding death…humans will understand that death does not exist. They will know that our opportunity to learn and to grow is never over; and that the time to be rewarded or punished for how we lived our lives will never come, because life is not a Reward & Punishment proposition, but rather, a process of continuous and unending growth, expansion, self-expression, self-creation, and self-fulfillment.

Death will be understood to be simply and only a transition—a glorious shifting in the experience of the soul, a change in our level of consciousness, a freedom-giving, pain-releasing, awareness-expanding breakthrough in the eternal process of evolution.

One result of this teaching: Many humans will know that death is not something to be feared, but a wonderful part of the wonderful experience called Life Itself.

People will talk about death freely and without undo sadness. People will not feel compelled to cling to life when they are suffering and dying, because they'll know that there is nothing BUT life, and so there is no reason to cling to The Only Thing There Is.

> Death is not something to be feared, but a wonderful part of the wonderful experience called Life Itself.

Endless suffering at the conclusion of one's time in a particular physical form will no longer be demanded or required as a matter of spiritual integrity, any more than it's required of other life forms.

This does not mean that ending one's own life as a means of escape from particular difficulties or sadnesses will be or is encouraged. It will be understood that life in one's present physical form is a wondrous gift, and no one will ever wish to toss it away in order to sidestep its challenges, but will understand at the deepest level that it may be used in order to experience who we really are.

In this and in many other ways, personal lives will be remarkably different when humans create a New Cultural Story.

With apologies and an honoring of John Lennon…

Imagine…personal relationships with all others that are no longer need-based, but emerge more profoundly from an experience of personal fulfillment, personal power, and the personal expression of the highest thought about yourself and others that resides within everyone!

Imagine…romance that exudes not from the thought that you "can't live without" someone, but from the awareness that the expression and experience of your fullest and highest and grandest Self is not dependent on any other person, but enriches every person whose life you touch immensely, allowing you to truly love from a place of giving!

Imagine…a career and work that feels more like joy and the celebration of the highest and best within you, and the happiest experience of Who You Are!

Imagine…a life without fear of God and without guilt over the tiniest infraction of what you imagine to be God's Rules!

Imagine…the freedom of soul and mind and body that would be experienced when you understand at last that you really *are* One with God! Imagine the power that you would experience—the power to create the life of your dreams, and to assist others in creating theirs!

Imagine…the end to frustrations and anxieties and worries about tomorrow, to say nothing of the sadness and bad feelings that can't seem to be shaken about things that happened yesterday, when you realize that *nothing can go wrong,* that all things are perfect just as they are, that God does not require anything different from you except exactly what you are being, exactly what you are doing, and exactly what you are having right now!

Finally, imagine…experiencing the awe and wonder of life, expressing through you AS you in your day-to-day moments, because of your wonderfully expanded awareness.

This is just a taste of what life could be like in the days of the New Cultural Story, and you don't have to wait for all of humanity to create that experience collectively. All people can begin to create it individually for themselves, and in the lives of those whose lives they touch. That is, in fact, what life invites you to do! It's what God is *calling* you to do right now.

You may begin *this minute.*

POINTS I HOPE YOU WILL REMEMBER...

• The time for courage has *really* come.

• Oneness is the basis of our New Cultural Story.

• There is nothing that is not part of The One Thing That Is.

• No human beings need ever be afraid of God again.

• There is no form and no manner in which the expression of a love that is pure and true is inappropriate.

• God does not want anyone to suffer, ever.

• Death does not exist.

ACTION I HOPE YOU WILL TAKE...

• Share the ideas you see here about how life could be if humanity only embraced a New Cultural Story.

• Add to these ideas yourself by contributing your inspirations at *www.TheGlobalConversation.com.*

• Please read my previous book, *What God Wants* (2005, Atria Books), in which many of these ideas appeared. This book should be on your Must Reading List—and is highly recommended by me as the one book I would give first to anyone who asks about the *Conversations with God* material and may want to know more about it.

THE MYSTERIOUS 'THIRD THING' THAT CAN CHANGE OUR WORLD

CAN YOU IMAGINE A new story for all of us to live and to teach our children based on those ideas? I get so excited about it, I can't stand it! But now I want to share with you some mechanical information. I mean, there are some mechanics in the Universe that we all need to know about if we want to put a daring new story into place.

So let me tell you now about a great secret that reveals itself in all of Life, *but only upon the closest examination.* And you'll see, in just a very short while, how this relates to our entire conversation.

Should we choose to overlay the secret I'm about to tell you upon humanity's Cultural Story, everything suddenly makes sense, and we suddenly have a formula, a mechanism, an approach to the living of human life *that works.*

Indeed, it is our failure to *live this secret* as part of our Old Cultural Story that has turned our Story from a dream into a nightmare. The revealing of this secret, and the placement of it at the foundation of our New Story, will turn our long global nightmare back into a dream again.

And no…this particular secret is not The Law of Attraction. This not-immediately-apparent aspect of life is what I have come to call The Secret of Three-in-One. It has been unveiled for us in *Conversations with God.*

All things are One Thing, says *CWG*, and everything *in* the One Thing is divided into three parts.

Everything.

At first glance (which is the glance that most people use when viewing the world), it looks as if everything is divided into *two* parts. We appear to be living in a dyad. In fact, all is a triad. When we do not see it that way, we experience a distorted reality.

God is One Essence, divided into three—what certain theologies call Father-Son-Holy Spirit.

Humans are One Being, divided into three—Body-Mind-Spirit.

Time is One Moment, divided into three—Past-Present-Future.

Space is One Place, divided into three—Here-There-In Between.

There is only One Place, One Moment, One Being, and One Essence. The Whole of All is Divided into Three Expressions.

What does this have to do with Humanity's New Cultural Story?

Everything.

It is the shift we will make within our story, from a dyad reality to a triad reality, that is going to change our entire experience.

The problem with how we are living our lives right now is that we see things mostly in two's. We see male-female, good-evil, up-down, fast-slow, big-small, hot-cold, black-white...and on and on. We see dyads where there are triads.

> It is the shift we will make within our story, from a dyad reality to a triad reality, that is going to change our entire experience.

When we see triads—when we see male-female-both, good-evil-both, up-down-both, fast-slow-both, big-small-both, and so on—then we realize that while a thing appears to be either good *or* bad, in reality it is *both* at the *same time*, which is a third thing altogether. While a thing appears to be either up or down, in reality it is *both* at the *same time*, which is a third thing altogether. While a thing appears to be either fast *or* slow, in reality it is *both* at the *same time*, which is a third thing altogether.

Let me repeat that, in just a little different way, because this is very, *very* important.

This is about seeing the dyad *together*, rather than as *separate elements*. In other words, we stop seeing *either* This *or* That, but *both* This *and* That simultaneously—which is a Third Thing Altogether. That is, it is a Third Thing...*All Together*.

This mysterious Third Thing is *so* mysterious that we don't even have a word for it. We are so used to conceiving of our world as a dyad that we have not created a way to talk about this Third Thing. We even doubt that such a thing exists. We wonder, how can two things be a third thing called *both?*

Simple. Point of view.

It depends on how you look at it.

The definition of *everything* depends on how you look at it. Nothing is as it seems, and the moment you change your perspective you see that. Therefore, there is no such thing as Reality; there is only the reality *you create* by the way you are *looking at something*. You are *creating* your reality through the use of *perspective.*

So, it turns out that this mysterious Third Thing is really only One Thing, divided into three parts. A thing is either good or bad—or something in between. A thing is either up or down—or something in between. A thing is either fast or slow—or something in between. It is the *in-betweenness* for which we have no word.

Or do we?

Don't look now, but I've just described the Triune Reality that is the One Thing that some of us call God.

The Roman Catholic Church teaches this exact theology. It speaks of a Three-in-One God, called The Holy Trinity. There is much in Catholic doctrine with which I do not agree, but this is one message that cuts right to the core of What Is So.

A thing is neither "good" *nor* "bad," it is something in between—and it is that *in-betweenness* that holds both "good" and "bad" in place, and makes the experience of them possible. And making the experience of God possible by creating the illusion of "not God" possible, through the producing of a contextual field within which Divinity can be fully realized in relative terms, is *the way that life works.*

Our world of duality is created by the Triune Reality of God, so that Divinity Itself may know Itself in Its own experience.

What we have done here on Earth is produce the illusion of a dyad out of the reality of a triad, and in this way we have created duality— including the greatest duality of all: Life and Death.

You see, only a triad creates the possibility of a continuum. A dyad cannot. Try to get that. Try to picture that in your mind. Draw a line that creates a dyad. You have one thing "over here" and another thing "over there." You can only go back and forth along the line. *You cannot continue going forward.* You cannot endlessly move in one direction because sooner or later you reach the end of the line. Then you have to double back. You have to turn around and go the other way. That's the problem with dyads—and with a dyad world. It violates the first principle of evolution. Evolution moves forever *forward.*

Now draw a second line in your mind. Let this connect three points. Now you have a triangle. Now you've created eternity.

Along this line you can move endlessly forward. You will visit the same places you've visited before, but you haven't gone *back* to them. You've encountered them *again*—and that is not the same thing at all.

This is what you do in your life. In your *endless life.* However, using your *endless imagination*, you have imagined that you can actually reach the end of a line that has no end. You call this "death." You say you have reached "the end of the line." But once you get there, you see that the line does not end. It merely turns. It goes up, up, up to The Third Point.

> The journey never ends. It never, ever, ever ends.

That is where we all go. And then, after remaining a while, we come down the other side of the triangle. We are, in human lingo, "on the other side." We slip down quietly, reaching the *beginning of the line*, and then we travel the baseline between what we call Birth and Death all over again. Some people call this *reincarnation.*

The journey never ends. It never, ever, ever ends. The trick to making the journey a joy is to understand what is actually happening, to understand the nature of ultimate reality. All things are One Thing. There is only One Thing, and all things are part of the One Thing There Is.

Yet in this physical reality, this world of our illusion, we do well to think in terms of Three Things in One—the Holy Trinity. We do well to get out of our dyad world and into a triad reality; to embrace what I call The Triune Truth: a thing is neither *this* nor *that*, but a Third Thing altogether. The Third Thing that's the One Thing.

Are you getting this? Are you stringing all this together?

I hope you are, because this all has to do with our New Cultural Story, and what it will tell us and our children and our children's children about Life and how it is. And that, my friends, will change everything.

Opening our vision

In the new World of Three we will see that it is impossible to be only male *or* female, but that the reality is, we are *both;* only fast *or* slow, but that the reality is, things are *both;* only black *or* white, but that the reality is, it is both.

It has been said that when we stop seeing things as either black or white and start seeing shades of gray, we have grown up. It is said that when we stop insisting that a thing is either "this" or "that," but that it can be "this" *and* "that," we have at last matured. It is said that when we shift from an either/or reality to a both/and reality, we become masters.

This is not only how we master ourselves, this is how we master our world.

Since *Conversations with God* showed me this, I have taken to saying things like, "Oh-oh, this is bad...unless it's not." "This is good...unless it's not." "This is just what I need...unless it isn't." "I can't do it...unless I can." "We're going to be late...unless we aren't." "I hate asparagus...unless I don't."

> Throughout all of life, everything is an expression of the One Thing That Is, in varying degrees.

Suddenly I found myself *open to the possibilities.* I mean, possibilities I never considered before. Not the least of these was the possibility that there might be something I don't fully understand about something, *the understanding of which could change everything.*

I began seeing things as *degrees* of the Only Thing There Is. I was given, by God in the *CWG* dialogue, an example I could use to help explain this to others: We describe any given day as either "hot" or "cold," whereas there in Only One Thing, called Temperature.

Throughout all of life, everything is an expression of the One Thing That Is, in varying degrees.

I suddenly began to see life in Shades of Gray.

What a growing up this was!

The most important part of the trick

Now once again you might say, "Yes, yes, very nice, very true...but what does all this have to do with our New Cultural Story?"

And I would answer once again, "Everything."

Then I would ask you to listen just a tiny bit longer. I would say that it would really benefit you to comprehend the *implications* of the fact that our dyad is not a dyad at all.

First, let me say that the way to deal with the fact that is life on Earth is an illusory experience is not to step outside of the illusion (that would defeat its entire purpose), but to live within the illusion *knowing* that it's an illusion.

The idea is to continue to perform the magic, but to remember that you are doing so. Or, as we have it from a somewhat more eloquent source, to be *in this world, but not of it.*

When we *know* that this whole experience is an illusion, we can work with the biggest illusion of all—the Illusion of Duality—in such a way that the illusion serves us, rather than getting in our way, as we seek to have the ultimate experience of life on Earth, both in our personal world as well as our collective experience.

For most of us, our personal world—what I call our Individual Life— has been lived primarily as if we were two-part beings, made up of body and mind. Our more outward experience—what I call our Collective Life—has been cut in two as well, with our most important and impacting group activities primarily made up of economics and politics.

Yet there's a third aspect of our Individual Lives that complements the body/mind dyad, and there's a third aspect of our Collective Lives that complements the economics/politics dyad.

We have not paid nearly enough attention to that Third Thing in our Individual Lives, which I am going to call the soul, and we have not paid nearly enough attention that Third Thing in our Collective Lives either, which I am going to call our culture.

Fascinatingly, this Third Thing is in both cases the most important thing of all. Why, then, have we not paid much attention to it? Because we have not *understood* its importance.

Only relatively recently, as the history of humankind is measured, have we begun to grasp the relevance—indeed, the *critical* relevance—of this Third Aspect of Individual and Collective Life. That awareness has finally come upon us only in these most recent millennia, and *full force* only in perhaps this most recent century, as part of our species' long evolutionary process.

We are, on the scale of the Universe, still a very young species. A lot of people like to think of humans as highly evolved. In fact, humanity has just emerged from its *infancy* on this planet. In their book *New World New Mind,* Robert Ornstein and Paul Ehrlich placed this in perspective in one mind-boggling paragraph:

"Suppose Earth's history were charted on a single year's calendar, with midnight January 1 representing the origin of the Earth and midnight December 31 the present. Then each day of Earth's 'year' would represent 12 million years of actual history. On that scale, the first form of life, a simple bacterium, would arise sometime in February. More complex life-forms, however, come much later; the first fishes appear around November 20. The dinosaurs arrive around December 10 and disappear on Christmas Day. The first of our ancestors recognizable as human would not show up until the *afternoon of December 31. Homo sapiens—*

> We are still a very young species.

our species—would emerge at around 11:45 P.M. All that has happened in recorded history would occur in the final *minute* of the year."

Did you get that? Did you feel the impact of that? Don't let that slip past you. Read that again if you have to, to let it really sink in. You've got to get this. You've got to know where we are in the overall scheme of things. Because this explains *a lot.*

Early in our process of growth as a species, human beings were like children, tending only to their most basic needs: (a) getting things done that helped them stay alive (later shaped into something called "economics") and (b) getting others in their clan or tribe to *help them* stay alive (later constructed as "politics").

Having noted that, I like to think that we're now living the last seconds of that final minute. We are approaching Midnight in the Garden of the Gods.

My dear, wonderful friend and colleague Barbara Marx Hubbard calls December 22, 2012 "Day One." She is absolutely convinced that this is the day of our true birth into the cosmic community of evolved sentient beings—and that the time up until now has been, figuratively speaking, our species' gestation period.

(If you would like more on this remarkable woman and her breathtaking insights into Life and Tomorrow, you will immensely enjoy *The*

Mother of Invention, her biography, which I had the great good fortune to write, and which is, truly, the story of us all.)

How evolution brings revolution

Because we are now a tiny bit more evolved, we are no longer devoting all of our time to our most basic needs: (a) getting things done that help us stay alive ("economics") and (b) getting others around us to help us stay alive ("politics"). We are now becoming concerned with (c) that Third Thing: *quality* of life (what might loosely be called our "culture").

And this is foundationed in our culture's *story*: our most sacred and valued myths about who our God is, what our social rules are, how we live together as a community, what we believe, why we marry, how we create families…even how we make music, what we sing, when we dance, what we call art.

This is the soul of us, and when we began to discover, as we evolved, how important this was to us, we began not being very happy with living a two-level existence—either in our Outside *or* our Individual Lives— nor with what that two-tiered formula has produced.

And so we've had revolutions. And more revolutions. And then, still more after those, all over the world. And conflict not just *within* countries, but *between* countries. Because while our politics were a *little* different (we all wanted the same things, though we went about getting them in different ways), and while our economics were a *little* different (we've had many ideas on the earth of how economics should be dealt with, but we all have wanted the same basic results), our *cultural* stories have been widely, *widely* divergent.

From country to country we've all tried to use our local economic system to get us what we need to stay alive. From country to country we've all tried to use our local political system to produce the cooperation we need to help each *other* stay alive. But when there came a growing awareness of the part of life that we weren't paying that much attention to before, we saw how different we were *culturally* from each other, and we found ourselves unable to avoid a "clash of civilizations."

This clash has produced flash points around the world for decades, and increasingly since the turn of the century. It was predicted in a thesis on the post-Cold War new world order originally proposed by the late political scientist Samuel P. Huntington.

The theory was formulated in a 1992 lecture at the American Enterprise Institute, which was then developed in a 1993 article in the journal *Foreign Affairs* titled "The Clash of Civilizations?" in response to Francis Fukuyama's 1992 book, *The End of History and the Last Man.* Huntington later expanded his thesis in a 1996 text, *The Clash of Civilizations and the Remaking of World Order.*

(Source: *http://en.wikipedia.org/wiki/Clash_of_Civilizations*)

And so we see now, internally within nations and externally between countries, the people of Earth are tired of the way life is.

I mentioned very early in our conversation that we need to be clear about that. We need to understand that dissent—including violent dissent—is going to continue all around the world until things get better.

I said that what I am seeing everywhere is that the human race is losing patience with itself. We do not *want* the kind of world we've created.

Like a dissatisfied artist standing back from the canvas, we've decided that we're not pleased with the picture we've painted. And so we're warring with ourselves and we're warring with each other—*because we don't know what else to do.*

You see? We thought it was a political problem. Then we thought it was an economic program. Those were the only two things that we seriously considered, because *we thought our Collective Life was a dyad.* And it's only occurred to us lately that it's not about that dyad. It's about the Third Thing that makes the triad.

And because more and more of us see this, it's become very clear that we can't paint a better picture by using the same brush strokes in the same places with the same colors we used before.

Something's got to change.

It's time to tear up the canvas and start over.

It is this awareness that is producing the Overhaul of Humanity.

It is what has happened as a result of our species maturing, and thus seeking, yearning, and demanding now to bring our *culture* into the equation with our economics and our politics.

It is no longer acceptable to most of us to simply be trying to make a living and get others to help us stay alive. Humans now want to make a *life* rather than a *living.* And this is making all the difference in the world.

I mean that literally. I mean, it is making all the *difference* in the world.

Now…my dear and wonderful friends…if we don't keep up with that difference, with that shift in humanity's overall priorities from survival in life to quality of life…we're going to find ourselves at the *effect* of, rather than at *cause* in, the Overhaul of Humanity.

POINTS I HOPE YOU WILL REMEMBER…

- All things are One Thing, and everything in the One Thing is divided into three parts.

- The journey of life never ends.

- The way to deal with the fact that life on Earth is an illusory experience is not to step outside of the illusion, but to live within the illusion knowing that it's an illusion.

- Humans now want to make a *life* rather than a *living*. This is making all the difference in the world.

- We are approaching the day of our true birth into the cosmic community of evolved sentient beings.

ACTION I HOPE YOU WILL TAKE…

- Look at your world closely and see if you can identify any dyads that are really triads. When you notice one, explore in your mind what The Third Thing is, and what your experience of this item in life would be if you wrapped that Third Thing into your considerations of it.

- Decide now to become part of the process by which all of us rewrite the Cultural Story of humanity. Place before our species a new set of beliefs that will produce a new set of behaviors that will bring *into the equation*, and bring into *balance*, our *Culture* as well as our Economy and our Politics.

A COMPLETE SHIFT IN
THE WAY WE 'DO LIFE'?

I HAVE SAID SINCE the outset of this conversation that there is nothing for us to be afraid of in the years ahead…save doing nothing. Then I have given all of us *something to do*, so we didn't have to worry about doing nothing. Now we had something we can all do easily. We simply needed to engage people in conversation.

I have suggested the topics for these conversations. I have said they might revolve around Seven Simple Questions. And finally, I promised to offer some beginning ideas as the basis of opening discussions around the creation of humanity's New Cultural Story.

Now to keep that last promise…

My wonderful fellow human beings, I am proposing here a complete shift in the way we live our lives, from a dyad to a triad reality.

This is not a new idea. Actually, it's a rather old one. Nor am I the only one proposing it in these new times. Which is what tells me that it's a very *good* idea.

Let us speak first about our Collective Life (the life we experience exterior to ourselves; our experience as a civilization), then, a bit later on, we'll look at how shifting from a dyad experience to a triad experience would work in our Individual Life (the life that we experience interior to ourselves; our experience as an individual).

Innovating our society's future

Others, far more credentialed than I will ever be, have been talking for a very long time about humanity's global experience and how it could shift. I believe that now it is time for all of us to be talking about it, and so…these opening thoughts for our New Cultural Story.…

I first heard of the idea of balancing spheres of our Collective Life when I became familiar nearly 20 years ago with the thinking of Rudolf Steiner, an Austrian who lived from the latter half of the 19th century to the first quarter of the 20th, and who was variously described as a philosopher, social innovator, architect, and esotericist.

In recent times I have been brought back to the idea again, through an awareness of the work of Nicanor Perlas, III a social activist from the Philippines and the 2003 recipient of the Right Livelihood Award (often referred to as the "Alternative Nobel Prize").

Let me go back to that first connection.

It was Rudolf Steiner who proposed that in an enlightened civil society there would be a natural experience and expression of three areas of endeavor: Economy, Politics, and Culture.

He also suggested that society could only function harmoniously when each was granted equal importance and sufficient independence to allow those three realms to "mutually correct each other in an ongoing process."

This idea became known as "social threefolding."

Prior to the end of World War I, an article in *Wikipedia* relates, Steiner spoke increasingly often of the dangerous tensions inherent in the contemporary societal structures and political entanglements. He suggested that a collapse of traditional social forms was imminent, and that every aspect of society would soon have to be built up consciously rather than relying on the inheritance of the past.

Anything here you can agree with?

Let me repeat that, because you may have glossed over it. Rudolf Steiner was predicting *a hundred years ago* that a *collapse of traditional social forms* (shall we call this our Old Cultural Story?) *was imminent,* and that *every aspect of society would soon have to be built up consciously* (shall we call this the Overhaul of Humanity?) rather than relying on the inheritance of the past (shall we call this the need to write a New Cultural Story?).

Now a hundred years, as we've just learned, is but the blink of an eye in cosmic terms. So Steiner's prediction that the overhaul was "imminent" was not that far off. (And, of course, the stock market crash and the economic collapse of 1929, producing The Great Depression, came breaths after his writings appeared, and was a harbinger of things to come just 75 years later.)

Taken from the *Wikipedia* article virtually *verbatim*, here's a rundown of Steiner's main points about Social Threefolding, upon which he suggested modern society be based.

> I am proposing here a complete shift in the way we live our lives, from a dyad to a triad reality.

(I'm presenting this *Wikipedia* article here because I believe what Steiner offered deserves our particular attention in these days just ahead as we consider how we might write our own new story.)

See if you agree with Steiner's contention that we should create:

SEPARATION BETWEEN THE STATE AND THE ECONOMY (STAKEHOLDER ECONOMICS)...

Examples: A rich man should be prevented from buying politicians and laws. A politician shouldn't be able to parlay his political position into riches earned by doing favors for businessmen. Slavery is unjust, because it takes something political, a person's inalienable rights, and absorbs them into the economic process of buying and selling.

Steiner said, "In the old days, there were slaves. The entire man was sold as commodity.... Today, capitalism is the power through which still a remnant of the human being—his labor power—is stamped with the character of a commodity."

Steiner also advocated more cooperatively organized forms of capitalism (what might today be called stakeholder capitalism) precisely because conventional shareholder capitalism tends to absorb the State and human rights into the economic process and transform them into mere commodities.

SEPARATION BETWEEN THE STATE AND CULTURAL LIFE...

Examples: A government should not be able to control culture; i.e., how people think, learn, or worship. A particular religion or ideology should not control the levers of the State. Steiner held that pluralism and freedom were the ideal for education and cultural life....

Examples: The fact that churches, temples, and mosques do not make the ability to enter and participate depend on the ability to pay, and that libraries and some museums are open to all free of charge, is in tune with Steiner's notion of a separation between cultural and economic life.

In a similar spirit, Steiner held that all families, not just rich ones, should have freedom of choice in education and access to independent, nongovernment schools for their children.

Steiner's view of education's social position called for separation of the cultural sphere from the political and economic spheres, and meant that education should be available to all children regardless of the ability of families to pay for it and, on the elementary and secondary level, should be provided for by private and/or state scholarships that a family could direct to the school of its choice.

Steiner was a supporter of educational freedom, but was flexible, and understood that a few legal restrictions on schools (such as health and safety laws), provided they were kept to an absolute minimum, would be necessary and justified.

Looking to the French

Steiner held that the French Revolution's slogan, *Liberty, Equality, Fraternity*, expressed in an unconscious way the distinct needs of the three social spheres:

- Liberty in cultural life,

- Equality in a democratic political life, and

- Solidarity in economic life.

According to Steiner, these values, each one applied to its proper social realm, would tend to keep the cultural, economic, and political realms from merging inappropriately; and allow these realms and their respective values to check, balance, and correct one another. The result would be a society-wide separation of powers.

Steiner argued that increased autonomy for the three spheres would not eliminate their mutual influence, but would cause that influence to be exerted in a more healthy and legitimate manner, because the increased separation would prevent any one of the three spheres from dominating.

(Source for most of the writing above:

http://en.wikipedia.org/wiki/Social_threefolding;

Re-use of material Licensing notice:

This work is released under CC-BY-SA. Here is the URL to the text of the license: *http://creativecommons.org/licenses/by-sa/3.0/)*

Advice not taken, predictions come true

Because society never adopted Steiner's model, each of those three spheres *has*, in one place or another on our planet during the ensuing years, *not* been prevented from dominating. His prediction of this was uncannily prescient.

Lack of autonomy had tended to make each sphere merge in a servile or domineering way with the others.

> We are talking here about *socially engaged spirituality.*

Among the various kinds of macro-social imbalance Steiner predicted, *all of which have come to pass,* were three major types:

- Theocracy, in which the cultural sphere (in the form of a religious impulse) dominates the economic and political spheres. (Iran?)

- State communism and state socialism, in which the state (political sphere) dominates the other two spheres. (Russia and its satellite socialist states?)

- Corporate capitalism, in which the economic sphere dominates the other two spheres. (The United States of America?)

The game isn't over yet

These developments notwithstanding, we have not come to the end of the game. During this time, as we experience the Overhaul of Humanity, we can—you and I—write a *new* story about how we want both Collective Life and Individual Life to be.

And now along comes a gentleman named Nicanor Perlas as one possible inspiration, essentially picking up 100 years later where Rudolf Steiner left off. Let me tell you a bit about this man, and then share with you some of the articulations of an organization he has created.

Nicanor Perlas is a modern-day social thinker of the first rank, consultant to many government and nongovernmental organizations around the world, and was a candidate for president of the Philippines in the 2010 election (he lost to the Liberal Party's Benigno C. Aquino III).

After the election he launched a new national/global project called MISSION, or the Movement of Imaginals for Sustainable Societies through Initiatives, Organizing and Networking.

The goal of MISSION *(www.imaginalmission.net)* is to create a new kind of civil society, where the quest for sustainability is grounded in social threefolding. He speaks constantly of societal transformation that is based on and emerges from *socially engaged spirituality and deep substantive inner change.* (Italics mine)

This, of course, is exactly what *Conversations with God* and The Conversations Movement is all about. We are talking here about *socially engaged spirituality and deep substantive inner change.*

Straying from first purpose

Mr. Perlas' model for tomorrow calls for "an economics of solidarity or associative economics and not an economics of competition."

I understand the words "economics of solidarity" to mean an economic system that serves the *first purpose of economics.*

Originally, the purpose of economics was not to make a profit. The original purpose was simply to establish a system under which people could trade with each other, exchanging their goods and sharing their abilities, so that the entire community could survive.

The thought was that mutual benefit would create solidarity within a community, thus facilitating the entire group in marching toward its survival goal. A little like ants in a colony—to use an admittedly rough and somewhat lacking analogy.

No one imagined at the outset that the simple rules for trading goods and services would evolve into a system producing wildly disproportionate benefit for one sector of the community over the other—much less at the *expense* or on the *back* of the other.

That would not have been an economics of solidarity, but an economics of disunity and separation—which is precisely the economics of today, producing its Haves and its Have Nots.

Nicanor Perlas' call for an economics without competition could have come straight out of *Conversations with God*, which made the case in the mid-90s that competition was based on the concept that there is "not enough" of whatever it is we think we need to be happy—a concept that is almost bizarre in its degree of inaccuracy.

There is enough of everything we need for all of us to be truly happy, and all we have to do is find a way to share it. That's the outcome that economics was originally intended to produce. Sadly, somewhere along the way we *lost* our way.

Mr. Perlas suggests that we can get back to the First Purpose of economic activity, adding that under his proposal "…the concept of an open market will be retained, but price and profits as signals for economic decision-making will be removed from their central position.

"Instead, price and profits will be among the considerations for economic associations as they try to ensure that the human needs of all are adequately satisfied by the economic system."

The foundational thought here is that when the concerns of humanity's cultural sphere (what Nicanor Perlas refers to as "civil society") are given equal weight with its economic and political concerns, our Collective Life *works*—not just for the few, but for the many.

Says Mr. Perlas: "Some may think that societal threefolding is just a wonderful idea, but that's it, just a nice idea. In reality, aspects of it are already operational in the United Nations and other global institutions, as well as in the writings of prominent thinkers and leaders, including MIT Senior Lecturer Peter Senge, considered to be one of the top 5 business thought leaders of our time, as well as MIT's Otto Scharmer, founder of Theory U.

"There, they call it either 'tri-sectoral partnerships,' or 'global public policy network,' or 'societal learning.' In the end the idea is the same: the importance of mobilizing civil society, government, and business to achieve broad based, comprehensive sustainable development."

What do you think of this idea?

Okay, that's what imminent social thinkers have had to say about this idea of "social threefolding." I'd like to take a look at it just a little more closely now, in my own words, in so-called layman's terms—because I believe it could form an important part of the beginning foundation for humanity's New Cultural Story.

As I understand it in my regular-person way, "Threefolding" refers to a process by which society acknowledges, and *acts on its acknowledgment*, that everything people become engaged in or involved with during their daily Collective Lives falls into one of three main areas: the person's and the society's economics, politics, or culture.

To me, "economics" still means what we all do to survive—and the latter-day mechanisms that we've created (business, commerce, and industry) to allow us to do that. It is the process we have put into place by which we meet our needs and satisfy our desires.

"Politics" to me continues to mean all group or communal decision-making and governance that creates cooperation with, and assistance from, others. ("Cooperation with others" could mean laws that regulate communal and mutual behavior. "Assistance from others" could mean taxes that produce financial resources to then be used to assist those who need assistance; not just the poor, but anyone who requires assistance in the form of basic services—i.e., police and fire protection, water and sewer service, travelable roads and highways, etc.)

The word "culture" is a big one for me. I'm sure that's why Mr. Perlas likes the term "civil society." It is, perhaps, a term we can more easily get our hands around. I am going to wrap into this category all the things that people do besides (a) working for a living or (b) seeking cooperation or assistance from others. This could include activities related to spirituality, sports, entertainment, interactive social exchanges, meeting of basic human impulses (love, sexual expression, partnership, marriage, parenting, recreation, creative hobbies, etc.), and the ecology of our various planetary environments.

So now again, what Threefolding suggests is that life should be looked at as a threefold experience—and that none of these experiences should be dominated by any of the others. They should be kept separate, as far as normal and natural interactive life will allow, but interactive. *Separate but interactive.* That's the key.

I also understand proponents of Threefolding to be saying that because society has not embraced this model, single-sector domination continues to occur—and that this is the reason for many of the social ills and dysfunctions of today.

To me that appears to be an unassailable assertion.

Nobody could seriously argue the fact that corporate money and business influence dominates our politics. Nobody could deny that religion and religious views seriously impact our politics as well. Nor could anybody miss experiencing that business and the economy dominates our culture. All they'd have to do is watch 30 minutes of television on any given night. Or see if they could catch a good movie anymore without also catching product drop-ins in every other scene.

A thought that the content of these forms of entertainment is not in any way affected by the economic platform on which they stand would be, to put it kindly, somewhat unsophisticated.

What I am joining Mr. Steiner, Mr. Perlas, and others in suggesting here is that the New Cultural Story that you and I can collaborate in writing should include not only separation of Church and State, but elimination of the domination of one sphere of human Collective Life by another. We could get a start in doing that by:

- Creating laws making corporate donations to political campaigns illegal.

- Keeping business and corporate lobbyists out of the halls of our legislatures and, as I said earlier, stop treating corporations as if they were persons under the law, giving them the same rights as individuals.

- Regulating the amount and type of advertising allowed in all media, and granting at least 20% of all media to advertising-free public creation and public access.

- Guaranteeing equal time for all points of view on all media outlets on major political, economic, and social issues of the day.

- Providing sufficient public funding for nonbusiness-sponsored and noncorporate-dominated mass communication, such as public television, etc.

This list could go on and on. In fact, I hope it will. I've deliberately limited specific ideas and suggestions here in order to allow you the opportunity to enlarge this list and expand on these proposals, free of further influence or content.

What must occur if Threefolding is to work

Now there is one thing that absolutely has to happen if a new balance is to be achieved between the three spheres of human Collective Life. The third sphere must be recognized. It must be equalized. It must be given its proper place in the triumvirate.

Right now our cultural, spiritual, social, ecological, and communal aspects of life are subordinated to the economic and political aspects. They are given short shrift by the media (which is economics dominated) and by the government (which is politics dominated).

> Nobody could seriously argue the fact that corporate money and business influence dominates our politics.

These days the imperative of politics and business is to *cut off* the free flow of ideas from the cultural sector (public broadcasting, free access Internet, etc.).

"In fact," says Nicanor Perlas, "global powers behind one-sided globalization are only too aware of its strategic importance and are *trying to hijack or co-opt civil society* as a third global power and harness this force for their own ends."

Ideas from the cultural sphere, or what Mr. Perlas calls civil society, that do not coincide with the thoughts and goals of business or government are therefore systematically minimalized and marginalized—as will be, no doubt, the ideas in this book.

Even the *call* for ideas from *outside* of this book will probably be described by the Establishment as a jejune approach to the solving of humanity's problems; a naïve and simplistic appeal at best.

> Stronger than all the armies is an idea whose time has come.

Yet the appeal is neither naïve nor simplistic, but the most powerful tool ever put into the hands of humanity: *conversation.* For it is as Victor Hugo is said to have written in his diaries: *Stronger than all the armies is an idea whose time has come.*

I believe that humanity now is desperately calling for new ideas, and desperately needs to be stronger than all the armies. Those new ideas must emerge in particular (but by no means exclusively) from the cultural sphere.

They must come from spiritual teachers and artists, from poets and philosophers, from educators and ecologists, from journalists and athletes and postal clerks and miners and traffic cops and nurses and waiters and musicians and cooks and cleaners and clerks and salesmen and housewives and househusbands and from…*Regular People Everywhere.*

That is to say, from you.

For balance to be achieved between humanity's three activity spheres there must also be not merely an acceptance of the cultural sphere, not only a recognition of it, but an *honoring* of its *importance.* Its various expressions should be funded by the other two sectors as a matter of law and policy and social obligation, not as a matter of largesse.

Right now we can't even get the public to provide sufficient funds for elementary schools, for heaven's sake. The concern of everybody is to lower their property taxes, even if it means lowering the quality of education.

We've created secondary schools in which the teaching of Business Math has been judged more important than the offering of Drama or Music (so-called *extracurricular activities* which are now all-too-often budgeted out of education programs. But just *try* to eliminate another "extracurricular activity"—sports. Oh, no, *never.* Not in a country of *Friday Night Lights.*)

We've created television networks where crass cartoon shows replete with juvenile jokes about flatulence are given more prime time exposure than biography programs about people who have immeasurably enhanced the human experience, or discussion programs about current affairs, or enriching programs about the marvels of our planet and its countless life forms. In fact, as I have noted, many want to now cut off public funding for such programs altogether.

We have created a society in which an auto race is more important than the human race.

The U.S. government, through the budget of the National Guard, is reportedly spending roughly $20 million to sponsor NASCAR racer Dale Earnhardt Jr., while the Army spends $7.4 million to sponsor Ryan Newman, and the Air Force spends $1.6 million on AJ Allmendinger.

Apparently, according to press reports, the Army is spending another $8 million on NASCAR programs in general. All of this, the military says, is for the purpose of attracting new recruits.

> We have created a society in which an auto race is more important than the human race.

Not happy about this at all, U.S. Congresswoman Betty McCollum, D-Minn., proposed legislation that would ban the Pentagon from using taxpayer dollars to sponsor NASCAR race teams. Pretty wild idea, eh?

She issued a statement saying, in essence, that she found it beyond inappropriate for Congress to vote to spend multi-millions on race car teams while at the same time cutting funding for homeless veterans, community health centers, and family planning services.

I can't even believe this is a discussion. The Republican-controlled House of Representatives not only discussed it, but *voted down* McCollum's idea, 281-148.

Breaking the habit

As you can see, it's not going to be a simple matter to create an appropriate balance between the three spheres of Collective Life. As Nicanor Perlas notes…"Existing business and government powers often have to be forced to yield the cultural space that they long to occupy.

"These political and economic powers often need to be awakened *by a demonstration of cultural power* in order to appreciate the reality of civil society and the cultural realm.

"Because institutions are inhabited by people, there are such things as institutional habits. And problematic institutional habits often die hard and need to be countered by the activism of civil society."

The Conversations Movement is about just that. It is a manifestation of "the activism of civil society." It has been created precisely to create "a demonstration of cultural power," because "problematic institutional habits often die hard."

Part of the difficulty is that many people don't believe there really is a problem. Not a big one, anyway.

What about you? Do you believe that there's a major problem of imbalance today between meeting the needs of the people within our culture, the needs of the economic engine that was designed to sustain them, and the needs of it political machinery that was created to serve them?

Who is serving and sustaining whom?

POINTS I HOPE YOU WILL REMEMBER...

- What would be extraordinarily beneficial would be a complete shift in the way we live our lives, from a dyad to a triad reality.

- Society should be divided into three activity areas: economics, politics, and culture.

- Activities in these three areas should be interrelated, but never intermingled. Indeed, all efforts should be made to separate them, as they *are* intermingled now.

- What is needed in our world is societal transformation based on and emerging from socially engaged spirituality and deep substantive inner change.

ACTION I HOPE YOU WILL TAKE...

- Learn all you can about the concept of what is called "social threefolding."

- Bring this idea into your Seven Questions Discussion Group.

- Encourage the political, spiritual, and business leaders in your community to embrace threefolding as a construction concept in building tomorrow's world.

- Write letters to the editor of your local newspaper, snippets for internet social networking sites, blogs, and articles to submit to everything from church bulletins to magazines about the benefits of moving from a dyad (economics and politics) to a triad (adding culture, or citizens' lives) experience and reality in our collective and individual lives—then work for a balance between the three, rather than a domination by one.

Conversation #24

WHEN PLAYING BY
THE RULES IS UNFAIR

HAVE I BEEN OVERSTATING the facts here? I've been saying that when one sector or sphere of our Collective Life dominates the other two (as the economy is now dominating politics and culture), nothing can result but a dysfunctional society where the desires of the few are met at the expense of the needs of the many. Or where, if you please, the economy is served, but the mass of the people that the economy was *intended* to serve are not.

So, have I been overplaying the problem?

Let's see.

In late May, 2011 the Internet site *Truthout* published an interview of Thomas Pogge, who holds a PhD in philosophy from Harvard University and is the director of the Global Justice Program at Yale University. In the interview, Dr. Pogge provides an introduction to the world economic situation for those who may not be articulate in this area.

The interview was conducted by Keane Bhatt, an activist and musician in New York. Bhatt served in the Dominican Republic as a Peace Corps volunteer from 2008 to 2010.

In their exchange, Dr. Pogge pointed out that the collective income of half the world's population is *less than 3 percent* of global household income. Or, to use Dr. Pogge's exact words, "there is a grotesque maldistribution of income and wealth" on our planet.

When I discussed this recently in a small group one person said...

We all know that. I'm not sure I'd use the word "grotesque," but we all know there's a disproportionate distribution of income in the world. That's the nature of the beast.

I responded…

Is it, now…? Hmmm. Well, that's the very point we've been trying to make here. Yet you would not call this disproportion "grotesque"?

Look, life's not fair.

I agree. But that doesn't mean it *can't* be. At least, insofar as human-caused unfairness is concerned. "Acts of God" and all that are one thing, but we're talking here about stuff that *human beings do*. But okay, life's not fair, as you put it. Shall we see just how unfair it is?

> The collective income of half the world's population is *less than 3 percent* of global household income.

According to Dr. Pogge, the bottom quarter of the human population has only three-quarters of one percent of global household income. This is about *one thirty-second of the average income in the world*. On the other hand, the people in the top 5 percent have nine times the average income. So the ratio between the averages in the top 5 percent and the bottom quarter is somewhere around *300 to one*. How's that for unfair?

It's not the "fault" of those at the top, if that's where you're going.

Nope, I'm not going there at all. Because you're right. Responsibility for this situation must be carried on the shoulders of us all. And it's not a matter of "fault." How can we be faulted for living out our own culture's story? It is the *story* that's the problem.

"Given the total income and wealth available in the world today," Dr. Pogge says in the *Truthout* interview, "we could easily overcome poverty, which would require raising the share of the bottom half from three to roughly five percent."

Now you would think that wouldn't be so difficult, right? Not, I mean, in a caring society. But, says Dr. Pogge, "unfortunately, the trend is going in the opposite direction."

At one point in the exchange interviewer Keane Bhatt posed this question..."We're all familiar with assigning blame to an individual for hitting someone's car, but not with assessing the morality of the speed limit or lack of a stoplight. Are you saying that the rules themselves can be moral or immoral?"

Dr. Pogge offered an emphatic yes. And he used two well-known examples from human history to illustrate his point that the "rules of the game" (what I call our Old Cultural Story) are the problem. A case could be made that people are only playing the game according to the rules they've been given.

Slavery, for instance,

> Given the total income and wealth available in the world today, we could easily overcome poverty, which would require raising the share of the bottom half from 3 to roughly 5 percent of global household income.

is something we have all come to condemn. But were the people in America's Deep South who owned slaves unethical? Or is the law that *instituted and enforced legal property rights in persons* where the lack of ethics lies?

States should never have passed such laws, Dr. Pogge asserts, and "should not have been in the business of returning runaway slaves to their 'rightful owners.' The whole institution of property in human beings was an *unjust social institution* and should not have been maintained in existence." (Italics mine)

The second example Dr. Pogge offered was feudalism, an economic system where a few people own all the land and the others have no option but to be serfs on such a feudal estate. We now condemn feudalism, he goes on, and we condemn "the whole structure of rules that sustained feudalism."

Dr. Pogge urgently invites people to think similarly about the world economy.

"We should condemn as unjust a global economic order that leads to ever-increasing economic disparities."

But you said that responsibility for this situation is carried on the shoulders of all of us. Yet if we're "playing by the rules," how is that so?

I'll let Dr. Pogge answer, straight out of the *Truthout* interview:

"Governments and their hired negotiators are designing these supranational rules and pressing for their adoption and for compliance—and the US government first and foremost. These governments are elected by us, funded by us, acting on our behalf, sensitive to our will, and so, we are not mere bystanders observing the injustice."

Ah, so we circle back to a statement I made earlier.

The first belief we're going to have to change is the belief in our own "bystanderness."

Says Dr. Pogge: "To be sure, one citizen, or a few, may be powerless if all the rest are determined to benefit from the imposition of unjust supranational rules. But this excuse cannot work for large numbers. Just imagine 10 million US citizens saying in unison: 'I am just one powerless citizen. There is nothing I can do to change my government's policies'!"

That deadly poison—and the antidote

In the *Truthout* interview above (which is much longer in its original form--source: *http://www.truthout.org/yale-philospher-thomas-pogge-past-and-future-global-poverty/1303930954)* we see the perfect deadly mixture of two of the three spheres of human Collective Life: *economics* and *politics*.

> We should condemn as unjust a global economic order that leads to ever-increasing economic disparities.

So just what can a society that is so bound up in this paradigm do? Is there an antidote for this poison?

Says Dr. Pogge: "The key insight here is organization. Ordinary people like you and me can achieve very little on their own. We need to build support. Even if you are a thought leader and have some good ideas on how to make the world better, and even if you write five or ten books—that won't have much effect unless you have people who are willing to support your ideas."

Well, now…does Thomas Pogge start to sound a lot like Nicanor Perlas? ("…political and economic powers often need to be awakened *by a demonstration of cultural power.*") And so we have come full circle again. Everything that we are talking about here can be changed—if there are people who are willing to support new ideas.

In this case the ideas are going to be *your* ideas. *You* will be co-writing our New Cultural Story.

Yes?

POINTS I HOPE YOU WILL REMEMBER…

- There is a grotesque maldistribution of income and wealth on our planet.

- We could easily eliminate abject poverty in the world.

- Sadly, the trend is going in the opposite direction.

- We must lose the idea of ourselves as powerless citizens.

ACTION I HOPE YOU WILL TAKE…

- Build support in your community for the idea of searching for new solutions to humanity's problems.

- Start a discussion group around this notion.

- If starting such a group is not easy or convenient for you, be sure to at least pepper your conversations with others, wherever they might take place, with the thought advanced by Nicanor Perlas that political and economic powers often need to be awakened by a demonstration of cultural (and I'm going to add, spiritual) power.

- Again, bring all these ideas and thoughts to your places of interface with the Internet.

- Include in that not just social networking sites such as Twitter or Facebook, but The Conversations Movement site at *www.TheGlobalConversation.com.*

THERE'S NOT A THING WE CAN DO ABOUT ANY OF THIS

As WE GATHER WITH others to begin our conversations and to write our new future story, I wonder if we can agree on some common objectives. Here are mine. How do these line up with yours? For my part, I'm hoping that our new story will produce these outcomes...

1. An acceptance, at last, of the true identity of all humans as an aspect and an individuation of Divinity.

2. The embracing by more and more people— ultimately, millions—of the truth of the Oneness of all life and of humanity.

3. An understanding of why we are here upon the earth; a clarity as to the soul's agenda.

4. An end to abject poverty, to death by starvation, and to mass exploitation of people and resources on the earth by those in positions of economic and/or political power.

5. An end to the systematic environmental destruction of the planet.

6. An end to the domination of our culture by an economic system rooted in competition above cooperation and in the continuing quest for economic growth.

7. An end to the endless struggle for Bigger/Better/More.

8. An end to all limitations and discriminations holding people back—whether in housing, in the workplace...or in bed.

9. The providing, at last, of an opportunity—one that is truly equal—for all people to rise to the highest expression of Self.

10. Not the putting into place of social adjustments for the sake of "social correction," but as a living, on-the-ground demonstration of who we really are as a species.

The start of something big?

It's important to say now that I'm not talking about our world embracing socialism. I'm not talking about the relinquishing of individual responsibility in favor of a system where the State takes care of everything.

Neither, however, am I talking about pure and simple capitalism, where it's every person for him- or herself, the rule is survival of the fittest, and the slogan is "may the best one win" in an open marketplace of ruthless competition.

There ought to be a way to engender individual responsibility, make individual greatness possible, and guarantee collective well-being, all at the same time.

Well, am I not brilliant to be the first person to muse about *that* . . . ? (ahem)

Okay, so we've been pondering all this for a few thousand years. Okay. But we keep avoiding, we keep *assiduously* avoiding, the only area within human experience where the solution can be found: our *beliefs*.

Currently we believe that we are separate from each other. We also believe that there is an insufficiency of what we need to be happy. As well, we believe that we are other than, and not an individuation of, God (if we believe in a God at all).

But what if we tampered with these notions? What if we experimented a bit with this idea of who we are? And what if we embraced and acted on the belief that we and all other humans are part of the same being, even as the hand and the foot are part of the same body?

Mystics and spiritual teachers have been proposing these ideas for eons, and I've talked about them here over and over. Now imagine how exciting it would be if we all adopted these beliefs, and *applied* them in both our Individual Life and our Collective Life.

If I believed that you and I are One, would I treat you any differently than if my basic understanding is that we are separate from one another? If our Collective Life—our politics and our economics—was based on the idea that all of humanity was One, that every person is part of the same family and that our fates are not simply intertwined, but *interconnected*, would that have any effect on our group decisions, economic and political?

What if we chose, *as a species*, to adopt the beingness of singularity and of compassion? If that were our constant choice of Who We Are, can you imagine any of our individual or group behaviors changing?

Why, such choices might just create a whole new way for humanity to experience itself. And that experience might just be so magnificent as to motivate...can I say it?...a revolution. The Last Revolution.

Finding a name for this

So what I'm talking about here is not socialism. And it is not capitalism. It is not about changing our outer economic and political systems, but our inner emotional and spiritual understandings. This, *in turn*, would lead, quite organically, to a shift in our outward behaviors.

No, this is not socialism; it is not capitalism; neither is it humanism, nor even spiritualism. It's...

...*beingism*.

Hey, I had to coin a word. We've never experienced an Overhaul of Humanity on such a scale before, based on such a huge internal shift, so there's no word in the language for what we're exploring here. It's kind of a strange- sounding word, but it says what I want it to say.

"Beingism" is not based on a set of political principles or economic strategies. Beingism is based upon us *being* individually responsible and collectively compassionate simultaneously—out of our understanding and embracing of who we are.

I think we need to be clear about something as we move through the years just ahead. There's not a thing we can do about how the world is today. There's nothing we can do about how our global society is dominated today by the economic sphere. There's not a thing we can do about its injustices. There's nothing we can do about the state of our politics and the world that it has created.

> Humanity's most wonderful responses always reflect what is *desired*, not what is *required*.

I know that there is nothing we can do because we've tried everything. We do this and we do that, we do this and we do that, do this and do that all over again—and all we wind up with is a great big pile of do-do.

So I think we need to get that through our collective noggins. *There's nothing we can do* anymore.

What, then, you may ask, are all those "calls to action" in this book about? Ah, good question. My answer is that because our problems won't be solved by us trying to "do something about them" does not mean that we can't "be" something with regard to them.

We can. We can "be" caring, we can "be" compassionate, we can "be" generous, we can "be" tolerant and forgiving, we can "be" One With All Others—to offer just a few examples.

When what we are *being* changes, what we are doing will shift *automatically*. Our behaviors will *adjust themselves*.

Let me give you an example—a simple but vivid illustration—of how this works.

When you enter a funeral home, does your behavior change? Of course it does. Even from the car to the front door it starts to change. And once inside, its adjustment is complete and automatic, arising *out of the state of being* you have adopted; out of the unspoken inner decision you have made about who you are and how you choose to express that.

It is not necessary for those who run the funeral parlor to create rules and post signs about them. ("Speak softly." "Please be kind to the bereaved." "Do not steal the flowers." "Kindly shake hands and give hugs to relatives of the deceased.")

You know what's appropriate and you just do it.

Now suppose you made just such an unspoken inner decision about who you are in a larger context? Suppose the entire species made such a decision about *what it means to be human?* Would it be necessary for those who run the world to create rules and post signs? ("Speak nicely to people." "Please be kind to those who are suffering." "Exploitation of those who do not have economic or political power equal to yours is prohibited.")

No. Rules and signs would be obsolete. You would know what's appropriate, given who you are, and you would just do it. Laws wouldn't even be necessary. (*Conversations with God* tells us that laws are non-existent in highly evolved societies.)

The highest behavior arises out of *beingness,* not out of obedience. Humanity's most wonderful responses always reflect what is *desired,* not what is *required.*

So coming from "being" does not mean the abandonment of "doing." It means our doing is sponsored by a different Source.

When action is an expression of "being," it becomes a powerful demonstration of who we are.

When action is undertaken for "action's sake," it rarely achieves anything lasting. When action emerges as the natural expression of what one is *being,* such action impacts and changes the world.

The power of being can impact the world

Let's see how all this plays itself out in the real world.

The lady down the street (we'll call her Delores) decides there is something she must do—something she believes we all must do—for the poor, sick, orphaned, and dying children of the world. She has picked up a pamphlet somewhere and she is on fire. She wants to *do* something. Life has been good to her. She wants—and this is very sincere—to give back.

Delores manages to talk a few friends into working with her and they hold bake sales and get their kids to have car washes and they do whatever they can to raise funds and provide help for the children she wants to help.

Delores is coming from "doing." God bless her, she is "doing" some wonderful things. It will not, however, change much. She will touch some lives, and that is very special, and I want to thank Delores. She deserves our appreciative noticing.

Another lady is coming from *being*. She has embraced a notion of who she is that rises far above "doingness." It is an idea that she has about herself, not about what she can do.

She feels deep compassion in her heart and chooses to step into the *being* of that. *I am compassion,* she says. *I am God's emissary, God's deliverer of compassion and caring. I am that. This is Who I Am.*

She may not have said this in so many words, but this is the place of Pure Being from which she emerges. This *beingness* moves through her, *as* her, every time she sees a poor, sick, orphaned, or dying child. And she sees many. She is right where they are. She moves among them and ministers to them. She undertakes this mission not because there is something she feels she must *do*, but because there is something she deeply chooses to *be*.

> All change in life comes from within.

Out of this decision, she touches not just a few, but many. Others see what is happening, and they take up her work for her. Suddenly, with those others joining in, the reach of her efforts spreads around the world.

She becomes known globally as Mother Teresa.

No fair, you might say. She was a *saint*, for goodness sake. She had no husband or offspring. Delores couldn't be expected to drop everything and run off to personally care for the children of Calcutta.

No, she couldn't, and that wasn't the point I was making. But I was hoping to illustrate the difference in energy produced by the root cause, or the basis, of action. One action emerges from a desire to do something, one emerges from the desire to be something. Beingness produces an impact that doingness could only imagine. Beingness spreads the action like wildfire.

That is the point.

If we want to truly change the world, we cannot do it from the outside. Efforts to change our reality will include things we do, that's certain. But when those efforts start inside of us, as a burning desire to express an aspect of divinity that we choose to *be,* they inevitably produce doingness that touches many, many people. Why, it may even reach around the world…

Hot dog! We finally *get* it

Let me tell you about the New Age Hot Dog Vendor on Coney Island. Perhaps you've heard of him. He goes around saying to people, "I'm the New Age Hot Dog Vendor. Let me make you one with everything."

People smile and say, "Okay, make me one with relish, lettuce, onions, pickles, mustard, and catsup." He does, then hands it to them. Then he charges them a crazy amount, like $7.77, so that no one can hand him precisely what he wants. When they give him a $10 bill, or two 5's, he thanks them, turns and wheels his cart away.

"Hey!" the people inevitable say, "where's the change?"

"Change," the vendor announces, "must come from within."

The outside starts on the inside

All change in life, including change in our Collective Life, comes from within. And if our Individual Life is experienced as a dyad rather than a triad, we're going to have trouble creating a Collective Life change. For it is what's in humanity's soul, not what's in humanity's wallet, that will purchase our freedom from humanity's suffering.

I'm proposing in this conversation that humanity embrace itself, create itself, express itself, and experience itself based not upon principles guiding what we choose to *do,* but upon ideals guiding what we choose to *be.* Doing is an outside thing; being is an inside thing.

It is not my intention to propose a whole new social system, but rather, to place before humanity a possible *basis* for such a new system, creating—with co-authors from around the world—a proposal for a new set of *beliefs,* a new *cultural story,* from which a whole new way of being human, collectively and individually, may quite spontaneously emerge.

That cultural story will contain some new foundational principles to be sure. But mostly it will revolve around a reignited inner commitment to have life come *from* us, not *to* us.

I am going to suggest that this is the guiding principle of *Beingism.*

The idea here is to think about who we believe we *are* and who we choose to *be* before an event (such as the death of more children on the planet from starvation) happens, rather than after it has occurred. I have seen evidence that this can impact in a positive way the occurrence itself.

Indeed, by this simple but elegant method we can re-create ourselves anew in the next grandest version of the greatest vision ever we held about Who We Are, both as individuals and as a collective.

So, then, we are clear, yes? I am not proposing a whole new social order. I am proposing a whole new mental construct. It is changes in *belief,* not *behavior,* that I'm after. Provide the first and you'll produce the second.

The difficulty with humanity's previous attempts at reinventing itself is that we've always started with behaviors rather than with beliefs.

We continue to do so.

It is *beliefs* that allow 400 children to die every day of starvation on this planet. It is *beliefs* that cause one-third of the world's people to be destitute. It is *beliefs* that sentence millions to live in domination.

In the past the call has been to reform the way we act, rather than the way we think. The urgency has been to shift our *responses* to life, rather than our *basis* for life. Yet there is only one way to meet the challenges facing humanity:

We must alter, not the way we *conduct* ourselves, but the way we *construct* ourselves.

What kind of society are we building? What kind of future are we assembling? How are we teaching our children to form themselves? Are we telling them who they really are, and building them up for the experience of that? Or are we focused not on the *construction*, but on the *destruction*, of our highest ideals about life and the highest thoughts we've ever had about ourselves?

I shall say again, and shout it from the rooftops: We must choose not what we will *do*, but what we will *be*. For all "doingness" proceeds from "beingness," it is not the other way around. The devastation of humanity has been that we thought it was. *We thought it was the other way around.*

We have completely and totally mixed up the Be/Do/Have Paradigm, and this has been the single most damaging misunderstanding within the entire human experience.

Life's most important choice

What you choose to *be* during the Overhaul of Humanity is the most important choice you will make. You will make it not once, but thousands of times. Your choice will affect your whole life. Both your Individual Life and your Collective Life.

You are deciding on a minute-to-minute basis what you choose to be. You can decide this ahead of time, you can decide this in the here-and-now, or you can decide this after any moment has passed.

You can decide this consciously or unconsciously, but you cannot sidestep the deciding. It is either happening automatically, as a response, or intentionally, as a creation, but it is happening—continuously.

Most people choose what they are going to be unconsciously. They do it *without* intention, without purpose, without awareness. Beingness is, for them, a reaction they're experiencing, not an action they're taking. This is

> We must alter, not the way we *conduct* ourselves, but the way we *construct* ourselves.

because they think that what one is *being* results from what one is *doing*. They don't understand that it's the other way around.

Understanding all this thoroughly

The "Be-Do-Have Paradigm," then, is in summary a way of looking at life. It's nothing more or less than that. Yet this way of *looking* at life could *change* your life—and probably will.

It is precisely because what is true about this paradigm is that most people have it all backward, that when they finally get it straightened out and start looking at it frontward, everything in their life shifts 180 degrees.

Most people (I know I did) start out with the understanding that how life works is like this: Have-Do-Be. That is, when I *have* the right stuff, I can *do* the right things, and then I will get to *be* what I want to be.

When I *have* good grades I can *do* the thing called graduate and I can *be* the thing called employable…might be one example. Here's another. When I *have* enough money I can *do* the thing called buy a house and I can *be* the thing called secure. Want one more? Here goes: When I *have* enough time I can *do* the thing called take a vacation and I can *be* the thing called rested and relaxed.

This is how my father, my school, my *Old Cultural Story* told me that life works. The only problem was, I was *not* getting to *be* the things I thought I was going to get to be after I had all the things I thought I needed to have and did all the things I thought I needed to do. Or, if I did get to be that, I only got to be it for a short while.

> Where we're all coming from is where we're all going.

Soon after I got to be "happy" or "secure" or "contented," "relaxed" or "companioned" or "successful," I found myself once again *un*happy, *in*secure, and *dis*contented, *not* relaxed, *not* companioned, and *not* successful!

In fact, I wound up stressed, alone, and an utter failure, living as a Street Person for one solid year. No home, two pairs of jeans, three shirts, that's it. *That's it.*

So of course it seemed to me as if I did all that I "had to do" for nothing. It felt like wasted effort, and believe me, I resented it.

Then I had the conversations-with-God experience, and everything changed. God told me that I ended up in the wrong place because I'd started *out* in the wrong place. What I needed to do was *start* where I wanted to wind up. I was told to begin at the end.

All creation starts from a place of *being*, God said, and I had the Process of Creation reversed. The trick in life is not to try to *get* to be "happy," *get* to be "secure," *get* to be content (or whatever), but to start out *being* happy, *being* secure, *being* content, and *go from there* in the living of our daily lives.

Actually, *come from there*. It is a question of where you are coming from. Remember many years ago when young people used to walk around saying, "Hey, where are you coming from with that, man...?" Well, we're talking about exactly that. We're talking about where you're coming from. Because as we undertake the Overhaul of Humanity, where we're all coming from is where we're all going.

But really…can it *work*…?

Every audience I share this with "gets" all this as soon as I explain it. Eyebrows lift and smiles appear and the energy in the whole room lightens. (That's what I call "enlightenment!") But then somebody (thank goodness) is sure to ask, "How do you make this work if you don't *have* what you *need* to have in order to be what you wish to be?"

That's the entire room's question, and it's a fair one. Here's the answer I always give:

"The idea that there is *anything* you need to 'have' in order to be what you seek to be is false. *Beingness* depends on nothing—except your decision. You get to decide what you are, and no one gets to tell you otherwise.

"If you say you're happy, then you're happy. If you say you're secure, then you're secure. If you say you're content, then you're content. Who gets to measure these things if it isn't you?

"You are what you say you are, and your experience is what you say it is. It has nothing to do with what you have. Unless it does. That decision is yours. You can decide that it does or you can decide that it doesn't.

"Yet this much I can tell you. Coming *from* a state of being, rather than trying to get *to* a state of being, guarantees that the state of being is experienced *instantly*—for the simple reason that you are creating it arbitrarily."

So again, to cement it in…when you come *from* a state of being, you need to "have" nothing in order to begin the process. That's the beauty of it. You can have, literally, *nothing*. You simply select, like the Goddess and the God that you are, a State of Being, and then come from that place in everything you think, say, and do. You "act as if."

So if you choose to "be" compassionate or generous or forgiving or joyful, simply step into that. Because you're then thinking, saying, and doing only what a person who is *being* those things thinks, says, and does; you begin attracting the things that compassionate, generous, forgiving, joyful people have without effort.

The same is true of a society, or an entire species, that creates its reality in this way.

Like attracts like. This is a fundamental law of the Universe.

This is the Magnet of Creation. It attracts all the energies that create exterior and physical experience in the phenomenal world.

The Master Key

As we co-create our New Cultural Story, I hope we decide that *being-ness* is going to be its basic tenet, its foundational principle. Because who we are and who we choose to be is life's critical decision, and most people *go through their entire lives* and never think in these terms. Yet our New Cultural Story could invite people (and, most important, teach children) to think in these terms *all the time.*

Just you? What about the world?

Now whenever I talk about being vs. doing, people tend to see this as a very personal, singular, individual thing. It will help *them* to negotiate the times ahead, no question. But what about the others?

Yet the changing of not only your own life can be effected with this tool, but of life on Earth. If that were not true I would hardly spend this much time on it in a conversation about co-creating the Overhaul of Humanity by co-writing a New Cultural Story.

What I'm suggesting here is that the Conversation of the Century include not just discussions about economics, politics, and culture, but explorations of the *basis* of *all* life experience. That is the point of having those conversations revolve around the Seven Simple Questions. Once these questions are asked and answered, the stage will have been set, particularly with the last question, for the shift into *beingism.*

> Like attracts like. This is a fundamental law of the Universe.

One could decide that one is going to become—not a socialist, not a communist, not a capitalist, not a humanist, and not a spiritualist, but a *beingist.*

As a *beingist,* each piece of legislation in the halls of our governments, each business decision in the boardrooms of our corporations, each choice of words in the composing of our songs or the writing of our sermons or the making of our television programs or the creation of our movie scripts—every single action we take in every one of the three spheres of human activity—would be preceded by a courageous suggestion and a searing question:

"Let's take a look at what we are being here. Is this what we want to be?"

POINTS I HOPE YOU WILL REMEMBER...

- Humanity's New Cultural Story is not a call for a move to socialism.

- The new human will make a shift from Doing to Being in the living of life.

- When what we do emerges from a place of pure being, it can have an enormous impact on our world.

- Being can even be the source of all government actions, political choices, and economic decisions. When it is, the world will be transformed.

ACTION I HOPE YOU WILL TAKE...

- Enter into Beingness Training. Every day, every hour, if you can manage it, ask yourself one question: *What do I want to BE now?* It may be more than one thing. But just try one at a time for a while.

- Choose a State of Being (Happy, Compassionate, Sensual, Wise, Caring, Creative, Considerate, Forgiving, etc.) in advance of each approaching moment, then move into that. Make it a decision based on nothing. Allow it to be a decision made out of choice. *Pure choice.*

- Know that your experience of how you are being does not have to be a reaction to what is going on; it can be a *creation* of what is going on.

- Discuss this process with the members of your discussion group. Invite them to engage in the Beingness Training.

COULD WE EVER REALLY GET CLOSE TO ANYTHING LIKE THIS?

Now as you know, I've said that none of the ideas here are mine. All of them were inspired by God and were—how can I put this...?—*given* to me in the *Conversations with God* dialogues. The tool of beingness was one of the most impactful among them. I wondered, as I thought about how this concept might be overlaid on our global life, what it might ask of us. For instance, would *beingness* require a redistribution of wealth?

No sooner did my mind formulate the question than it received a reply.

"It would *require* nothing. It would *produce*, voluntarily and quite automatically, a redistribution of *resources*.

"*All* people would be offered a proper education, for instance. *All* people would be offered open opportunity to use that education in the workplace—to follow a career which brings them *joy*.

"*All* people would be guaranteed access to health care whenever and however needed.

"*All* people would be guaranteed they won't starve to death, or have to live without sufficient clothing or adequate shelter.

"*All* people would be granted the basic dignities of life, so that *survival* would never again be the issue; so that simple comforts and basic dignities were provided *all* human beings."

So this is how life would "be" if *we* chose to "be" compassionate and caring, generous and loving—and One with All People. But what if some folks did nothing to earn these things? I asked.

"Your thought that these things need to be *earned* is the basis for your thought that you have to *earn you way to heaven*," came the reply.

"Yet you cannot earn your way into God's good graces, and you do not have to, because you are already there. This is something you cannot accept, because it is something you cannot *give*. When you learn to *give* unconditionally (which is to say, *love* unconditionally), then will you learn to *receive* unconditionally.

"This life was created as a vehicle through which you might be allowed to experience that.

"Try to wrap yourself around this thought: People have a right to basic survival." Of course! If we are "being" One with all other humans, we would see that there could be no reason for people not to have the same right to survive that we assume for ourselves.

Yet there is a logistical problem here. Basic survival depends upon having the *means* to survive—and in an economy-driven world that requires a job, or some other manner of receiving income. Because without sufficient income, you're S.O.L. (Sure Out of Luck).

For example, you must certainly know that the food problem in the world today is not that there is not enough of it to go around, but that people can't *pay for it*.

This is the planet we're living on today. We are requiring people to *pay for their survival*—and if they can't do it, *we let them die*.

Why not a world in which we *guarantee* people's basic survival?

Couldn't we, as a caring society, offer that from our hearts?

I guess I'm just an old guy, still inspired by the words of the inaugural address delivered in 1961 by newly elected American president John F. Kennedy...

"The world is very different now. For man holds in his mortal hands the power to abolish all forms of human poverty and all forms of human life. And yet the same revolutionary beliefs for which our forebears fought are still at issue around the globe—the belief that the rights of man come not from the generosity of the state, but from the hand of God."

Ideas that provoke discussion

The problem of finding work enough for everyone seems simple enough to solve. Ask half of the working population to embrace early retirement. Offer them financial and quality-of-life inducements to do so. There would then be plenty of jobs for everyone else age 18 and up.

(By the way, companies use this tool all the time when it produces *economic* advantage. Could it not be done to produce *cultural* advantage?)

But what would happen to the "45-and-overs"? They would receive income for life from the World Citizens Fund. Money would be put into the fund by working people, who would each be taxed the exact same amount, 10%.

> Why not a world in which we *guarantee* people's basic survival?

There would be no evasion of this flat tax by anyone, first because everyone would think it was fair, and second, because each year newspapers and websites throughout the world would publish names of citizens within each community who chose not to pay the tax.

The "retired" folks, most with 25 years or more left in their prime, would contribute to their community and the world at large from their passions and their creativity and their skills, able—with their support until death no longer a worry—to offer all of their expertise freely and use all of their talents joyfully, enriching society unimaginably in the bargain.

This is just one simple (some might even say silly) idea. The larger point is that our species in the years ahead is going to be invited to decide what it wants to *be*.

Does it want to be a species within which the well-being of each of its members is held in the heart to be the joint responsibility of the collective as a whole? Or does it wish to be an every-man-for-himself species?

The first notion would not get much traction unless the society embraced the concept and announced: "We are all One."

The *Conversations with God* dialogue touched on a lot of this in Book Two. Here there is an interesting exchange in which I was pursuing the idea of everyone being taken care of by the community at large.

I asked, should all people have at least their survival needs met, even if they do nothing? I received an immediate response:

"Even if they do *nothing*. Even if they contribute *nothing*. Survival with dignity is one of the basic Rights of Life. I have given you enough resources to be able to guarantee that to everyone. All you have to do is share."

Being a pragmatist, I wanted to know what would stop people from then simply wasting their lives, lollygagging around, collecting "benefits." God's reply:

"First of all, it is not yours to judge what is a life wasted. Is a life wasted if a person does nothing but lie around thinking of poetry for 70 years, then comes up with a single sonnet which opens a door of understanding and insight for thousands of people? Is a life wasted if a person lies, cheats, schemes, damages, manipulates, and hurts others all his life, but then learns from it—learns, perhaps, something he has been spending lifetimes trying to learn—and thus evolves, at last, to the Next Level? Is that life "wasted?"

> Our species in the years ahead is going to be invited to decide what it wants to *be*.

"It is not for you to judge the journey of another's Soul. It is for you to decide who *you* are, not who another has been, or has failed to be.

"So, you ask what would stop people from simply wasting their lives, lollygagging around, collecting 'benefits,' and the answer is: nothing."

But wouldn't those who *are* contributing begin to resent those who are not? I wanted to know.

"Yes, they would," came the reply, "if they are not enlightened. Yet Enlightened Ones would look upon the non-contributors with great compassion, not resentment."

Compassion?

"Yes, because the Contributors would realize that non-contributors are missing the greatest opportunity and the grandest glory: the opportunity to create, and the glory of experiencing, the Highest Idea of Who They Really Are. And the Contributors would know that this was punishment enough for their laziness, if, indeed, punishment was required—which it is not."

I won't let go of an argument, of course (as those who know me will attest), so I found myself saying, "But wouldn't those who are really contributing be angry to have the fruits of their labor taken from them and given to the lazy ones?" The response was fascinating.

"First, nothing would be *taken* from them, because nothing would be given *to them* until *all* had been guaranteed minimal survival portions." In other words, a general tax for the welfare of all would first be deducted from earnings, just as it is today.

The difference is that under a New Cultural Story people would not see this as "taking from the rich and giving to the poor," or as "their" work supporting others, but rather, as the natural process that spontaneously emerges from a just and caring society. In such a society people would automatically think, "Of *course* we make sure that everyone can stay *alive* before we allow human beings to *die* while we worry about what luxuries we can afford."

Some people might still say, "Hey, we need a vacuum cleaner for each floor of the house—so our housekeeper doesn't have to carry one up and down, don't you see. I'm mean, they're heavy..." But most folks in a just and caring society would not let other people die of starvation while they purchased luxuries.

Yet, you might think, even with the basic needs of all being met, we would *still* have the "rich" and the "poor," just as we do today. That is true, but there would be, under such a New Cultural Story, equal *opportunity.* Everyone would have the *opportunity* to live a basic existence, without worries of survival. And everyone would likewise have an opportunity to have more; to acquire the knowledge, develop the skills, and use their natural talents in the marketplace in such a way that their income increases.

> Most folks in a just and caring society would not let other people die of starvation while they purchased luxuries.

And the responsibility (I should really say the "nature desire") to support such a system that would emerge from a New Cultural Story would be shared *equally* by all, rather than disproportionately by all. There would be no income tax of any kind. People will voluntarily *tithe* 10 percent of their income to what might be called a Fund for All.

If we tried to do this today, this would have to take the form of a so-called flat tax, because most of us are not sufficiently enlightened to see that voluntary deduction for the general good of all is in our best interest.

Yet when the shift in consciousness I have been describing occurs, such an open, caring, freely offered deduction from our harvest will be seen by us as simply appropriate. *We will know the appropriate thing to do, and we will do it.*

Such a completely voluntary tithe would be part of the "equal opportunity" offered by the New Cultural Story, offering all an equal opportunity to create a society that is just and caring.

The new story that would inculcate such a desire in people from their earliest years of childhood would be a story that teaches "We are all One," rather than "Survival of the Fittest." It would bring children the messages that "what I do for others, I do for me—and what I fail to do for others, I fail to do for me. This is true for the simple reason that there is only One of Us. We are the Same Essence, in multiple form."

Our schools would have to adopt an entirely new curriculum, of course, in order for such a concept to find a place in what we teach children.

(You may be interested to know that, while we await such a wholesale change in the curricula in our schools, individual home-schooling lessons have already been developed, with age-appropriate language and concepts, by The School of the New Spirituality. This material is made available in cooperation with the Youth & Family Ministry of the worldwide Unity Church. To learn more about how you may bring your children these messages, contact your nearest Unity Church or go to…

…*www.cwg4kids.com/unity*.)

Greatness trumps laziness every time

Right about now you may be thinking, *But what will guarantee that there would be enough Contributors to "carry" the non-contributors?* The answer is, the greatness of the human spirit.

Contrary to what some people seem to believe, the average person will not be satisfied with living at subsistence levels, and having nothing more. Certainly most of those raised within the New Cultural Story will not. A few will, but not most. In addition, all of the incentives in life will change when the second paradigm shift—the spiritual shift—takes place.

I haven't talked about this yet. We took a look here a bit ago at the first paradigm shift—the movement from a dyad to a triad in our experience of civil life—but we still have on our agenda the exploration of that same movement from dyad to triad in the experience of our spiritual life. We're going to take that up in our next conversation.

What would cause such a shift? It hasn't occurred already in the two-thousand-year history—actually, two-*billion*-year history—of the planet. Why should it occur now?

Because with the shift away from material survival (which will occur with the elimination of the need to "succeed" by someone else's standards in order to acquire even basic necessities), there will be no other reason to achieve, to stand out, to become magnificent, save the reason we all came to physicality to begin with—*to experience magnificence itself.* That will be sufficient motivation for almost any person, for we each have embedded within our DNA a natural impulse to greatness not for the simple sake of being "great," but for the

> The children of tomorrow will not be living our case of mistaken identity.

purpose of experiencing *divinity*—which is why we are here.

Whether we follow that impulse depends on our upbringing, but whether we have it does not. And children brought up within the New Cultural Story will feel and follow that impulse with excitement—for part of that new story will be a very clear description of who we really are and why we are here. The children of tomorrow will not be living our case of mistaken identity.

Is it possible to have 'more than enough'?

Now there is one more radical shift in how we may wish to "do life" that was proposed in that second volume of *Conversations with God,* and it's pretty radical (although by no means new), so we may want to take a look at it here before we close, if only for the stimulation of it....

I was told in that dialogue that under the new system we've been exploring for human society, everyone would earn as much each year as they could—up to a certain limit.

What limit? An arbitrary limit, agreed to by the people.

Anything above that limit would be tithed to a World Charitable Trust *in the name of the Contributor,* so all the world would know its benefactors. Those benefactors would have the option of direct control over the disbursement of 50 percent of their tithe, providing them the satisfaction of putting their money exactly where they want it to go. The other 50 percent would be allocated to programs selected by those chosen by the people through popular election to do so.

Of course, a universal cap on income is, as I just said, not a new idea. And it has raised many questions among all thinking people. For instance, if folks knew that all earnings above a certain amount would be taken from them, what would be their incentive to keep working? Why wouldn't they just stop in midstream once they reached their income limit?

The radical answer I got in the dialogue was: "Some would. So what? Let them stop. Mandatory work above the income limit, with contributions to the World Charitable Trust, would not be required.

> Gathering and *sharing* the wealth could not possibly produce the amount of human misery as gathering and *hoarding* the wealth has done.

"The money saved from the elimination of mass production of weapons of war would be sufficient to supply everyone's basic need. The 10% tax of all that is earned worldwide on top of those savings would elevate all of society, not just the chosen few, to a new level of dignity and abundance. And the contribution of earnings above the agreed upon limit (nonprofits could still ask for support) would produce such widespread opportunity and satisfaction for everyone that jealousy and social anger would virtually disintegrate.

"So some *would* stop working—especially those who saw their life activity as *real work*. Yet those who saw their activity as *absolute joy* would *never* stop."

Not everyone can have a job like that, I said. But God replied:

"Untrue. Everyone can. *Joy at the work place has nothing to do with function, and everything to do with purpose.*

"The mother who wakes up at 4 o'clock in the morning to change her baby's diaper understands this perfectly. She hums and coos to the baby, and for all the world it doesn't look like what she is doing is any work at all. Yet it is her *attitude* about what she is doing, it is her *intention* with regard to it, it is her *purpose* in undertaking this activity, which makes the activity a true joy."

Then God said something that caught my ear.

"The love of a mother for her child is as close as you may be able to come to understanding some of the concepts of which I am speaking."

Okay, so I was now being introduced to Unconditional Love as a concept in human social interaction and in humanity's economic, political, and cultural constructions. Add this to the *beingness* program and you have a planet full of sentient beings *being* unconditional love.

But I still could not see the purpose of eliminating limitless earning potential. Wouldn't that rob the human experience of one of its greatest opportunities; one of its most glorious adventures?

"No," said God. "You would still have the opportunity and the adventure of earning a ridiculous amount of money. The upper limit on retainable income could be very high—more than the average person . . . the average ten people . . . would ever need. And the amount of income you could *earn* would not be limited—simply the amount you would retain for personal use. The remainder—everything, say, over $25 million a year (I use a strictly arbitrary figure to make a point)—would be spent for programs and services benefitting all humankind."

As to the reason—the *why* of it—I was told that...

"The upper personal income limit would be a reflection of a consciousness shift on the planet; an awareness that the highest purpose of life is not the accumulation of the greatest wealth, but the doing of the greatest good—and a corollary awareness that, indeed, the *concentration of wealth*, not the sharing of it, is the largest single factor in the creation of the world's most persistent and striking political and social dilemmas."

In other words, gathering and *sharing* the wealth could not possibly produce the amount of human misery as gathering and *hoarding* the wealth has done.

Dismantling the greatest system ever?

Yet there are those who sincerely believe that the opportunity to amass wealth— unlimited wealth—stands at the cornerstone of a system of free enterprise and open competition that has produced the greatest society the world has ever known. What can be said to them?

Well, I would say what I was told in the *CWG* dialogue: that those who believe this are terribly deluded, and see nothing of the current reality on our planet. The interview with Dr. Pogge pointed to that reality in very clear terms.

I'll add to that here: In the United States, the top *one-and-a-half percent* own more wealth than *the bottom 90 percent*. The net worth of the richest 834,000 people is nearly *a trillion dollars greater* than the poorest *84 million people combined*.

So? They've worked for it, a person could say.

You see, many Americans tend to see class status as a function of individual effort. Some have "made good," so they assume that anybody can.

That view is simplistic and naive. It assumes that everyone has equal opportunity, when in fact, in America just as in other parts of the world, the rich and powerful strive to hold on to their money and their power, and to increase it.

> The guidance you are getting is to *follow your heart.* Listen to your *Soul.* Hear your *Self.*

What's wrong with that? Well, it's that they do so by systematically *eliminating* competition, by institutionally *minimizing* true opportunity, and by collectively *controlling* the flow and the growth of wealth.

This they accomplish through all manner of devices, from unfair labor practices that exploit the masses of the world's poor, to good-old-boy network competitive practices which minimize (and all but destroy) a newcomer's chances of entering the circle of successful companies.

They then seek to control public policy and governmental programs around the world to *further* ensure that the masses of people remain regulated, controlled, and subservient.

This is the point that Dr. Pogge made about exactly what is happening right now, and this is what Rudolf Steiner predicted 100 years ago *would* happen if the three spheres of human activity were not balanced, but rather, dominated by the economic sector.

Now it's important to make a point here, lest this portion of my conversation with you here starts to come off like a "rant" against the rich. It is not. I am among those who are personally wealthy. So I have a little experience with this business of being a person who is doing well.

I also know a lot of other people who are doing well. And here's what I understand. In most cases it isn't rich *individuals* who create the untenable and unjust situation I've just described. It's the social systems and institutions they represent.

Those systems and institutions were *created* by the rich and powerful—that includes me—and it is the rich and powerful who continue to support them. That does not include me.

By standing behind such social systems and institutions, individuals, without really thinking about it, are unconsciously washing their hands of any personal responsibility for the conditions which oppress the masses.

To offer just one example, millions of America's poor have no access to preventive medical care. One cannot point to any individual doctor and say "this is your doing; it's your fault" that in the richest nation on earth, millions can't get in to see a physician unless they're in dire straits in an emergency room.

No *individual* doctor is to blame for that, yet *all doctors benefit.* The entire medical profession—and every allied industry—enjoys unprecedented profits from a delivery system which has *institutionalized* discrimination against the working poor and the unemployed.

And that's just one example of how the "system" keeps the rich rich and the poor poor. The point is that it is segments of the rich and powerful who most often support such social structures, and who most often staunchly resist any effort to change them. Many people in this category (but certainly not all) stand against any political or economic approach which seeks to provide true opportunity and genuine dignity to all people.

Most of the rich and powerful, taken individually, are certainly nice enough people, with as much compassion and sympathy as anyone. But mention a concept as threatening to them as yearly income limits (even ridiculously high limits, such as $25 million annually); and a surprising number of them start whining about usurpation of individual rights, erosion of the "American way," and "lost incentives."

They declare that it's an infringement of freedom. So in the name of freedom they keep poor people in virtual slavery to an economic system in which the poor are "free" to barely survive.

Yet what about the right of *all* people to live in minimally decent surroundings, with enough food to keep from starving, enough clothing to stay warm?

What about the right of people *everywhere* to have adequate health care—the right not to have to *suffer* or *die* from relatively minor medical complications that those with money overcome with the snap of a finger?

The resources of our planet—including the *fruits of the labors* of the masses of the indescribably poor who are continually and systematically exploited—belong to all the world's people, not just those who are rich and powerful enough to do the exploiting.

And here is how the exploitation works: Our rich industrialists go into a country or an area where there is no work at all, where the people are destitute, where there is abject poverty. The rich hire a local company to set up a factory there, and the local company offers those poor people jobs—sometimes 10-, 12- and 14-hour-a-day jobs—at substandard, if not to say *subhuman,* wages. Not enough, mind you, to allow those workers to escape crowded and tattered villages, but just enough to let them live *that* way, as opposed to having *no food or shelter at all.*

And when they are called on it, some companies say (but not out loud), *"Hey,* they've got it better than *before,* don't they? We've *improved their lot!* The people are *taking* the jobs, aren't they? Why, we've brought them *opportunity!* And *we're* taking all the *risk!"*

Yet how much risk is there in paying people $1.25 an hour to manufacture products that are selling for many hundreds of dollars?

Is this risk-taking, or exploitation, pure and simple?

Such a system of rank obscenity could only exist *in a world motivated by greed, where profit margin, not human dignity, is the first consideration.* Those who say that "relative to the standards in their society, those peasants are doing *wonderfully!"* are hypocrites of the first order. They would throw a drowning man a rope, but *refuse to pull him to shore.* Then they would brag that a *rope is better than a rock.*

> It sure feels to me that you're biased against the rich,
> and opposed, as well, to the free enterprise system. It
> almost feels like you're making stuff up.

(This is another actual exchange I had on talk radio.)
Do you really think I'm doing that?

> Well, at the very least you're exaggerating. You're
> exaggerating to make a point.

It doesn't feel to me as though I am. I've seen press reports and news items all over the Internet from a dozen different blogs and sources about Apple, Inc.

Apple's own audits found labor, safety, and other abuses by its suppliers in 2010, including 91 underaged workers and *involuntary or debt-bonded labor* among other abuses found in audits of 127 production facilities.

The worst part about this: Apple allegedly tried to cover it up. It allegedly sought to keep details of its production difficulties a secret. These facts might never have come to light in any event, had it not been for a *string of suicides* at factories in China where iPhones and other devices are assembled.

My friend, I don't think this case is the exception. I think this kind of thing is happening all over the place.

> I don't know. It feels like the media is not the most reli-
> able source. I don't believe half of what I read in the papers
> or see on the news.

Yet the blogs and the TV news shows and the newspapers were all quoting Apple's own internal report.

(At this point the talk-show host cut in, saying that it seemed that the caller and I disagreed, and she went on with her show.)

These are starters, not enders

Okay, we've said some pretty edgy things here. If you're still with me, I know that at least you have an open mind. In the dialogue books I remember getting a little nervous about how this kind of talk, how these ideas, would go over in the larger world. Then I got a message that totally erased any unease I was feeling. That message:

"The guidance you are getting is to *follow your heart*. Listen to your *Soul*. Hear your *Self*. Even when I present you with an option, an idea, a point of view, you are under no obligation to accept that as your own. If you disagree, then *disagree*. That is *the whole point of this exercise.*"

"So...are there some answers to these purely political questions that you do not like? *Then change them.* Do it. Now. Before you start hearing them as *gospel.* Before you start making them *real.* Before you start calling your last thought about something more important, more valid, more True than your *next* thought."

That was a very important thing that was just said there, and I knew it when I heard it. I realized that this is exactly how our Old Cultural Story got to be so engrained, so powerful in our lives. We kept thinking that our last thought was our best. But I was told in the dialogue, "Remember, it's always your *new thought* that creates your reality. Always."

> The thoughts presented here are conversation starters, not conversation enders.

So please remember, the thoughts presented here are conversation starters, not conversation enders. This is just a place from which to begin a lively and vital dialogue. This is "the floor is now open," not "the discussion is closed."

Now while I obviously endorse the ideas offered here, I know that there are many people who do not. And there are some people in our world who will go to the opposite extreme. They think nothing of a socio-economic system that rewards a corporate executive with a $70 million bonus for increasing sales of a soft drink, while 70 million people can't afford the luxury of drinking the stuff. This is called, they will tell you, the world's Free Market Economy, and that's just how it works.

And you know what? That *is* how it works in a society whose engine is driven largely by economics, as ours is (for now). Yet I find this bit of writing striking...

"If thou willt be perfect,
go and sell what thou hast, and give to the poor,
and thou shalt have treasure in heaven."
But when the young man heard this,
he went away, sorrowful,
for he had great possessions.
—The Gospel according to Mark

BRINGING YOUR SOUL INTO YOUR LIFE: METHODS AND PROCESSES

WE'RE COMING TO THE end of our conversation here very soon, but before we do I promised that I would explore with you the transforming of the dyad into a triad in our Individual Life, just as we talked about Threefolding in our Collective Life.

So let's take a look at that.

I observe that most people think of their Individual Life as an experience and an expression of the body and the mind. There are not many people who think in terms of the experience and expression of their soul.

They may know that they *have* a soul, but they do not often (if ever) have an experience of it—and to talk in terms of having an *expression* of it seems almost like speaking in a foreign language of something they don't understand.

As with our Collective Life, our Individual Life is comprised of three spheres. And as with our Collective Life, if our Individual Life is out of balance, dominated by one of the other two spheres (body or mind), it's not going to be very fulfilling for us, or very meaningful.

The reason that the world is the way it is, and our individual lives are so difficult to live right now that they don't make sense much of the time, is that we're using only two-thirds of our three-part being. We have not learned to get in touch and stay in touch with our soul.

If we pay attention only, or primarily, to our body, we will experience our Individual Life as largely a physical experience, having not much purpose other than physical pleasure and physical survival.

If we pay attention only, or primarily, to our mind, we will experience our Individual Life as largely a mental experience, having not much purpose other than mental exploration and mental processing. Indeed, we will imagine that we are here on a Mission of the Mind. "I think, therefore I am," said Descartes, and many humans believe that life begins and ends there.

> We have not learned to get in touch and stay in touch with our soul.

I would want to turn around Descartes' famous statement and make it: "I am, therefore I think."

I am...*what*...though? That is the question. *Beingism* offers an answer. *I am what I say I am. I am what I am being, right now.*

This level of life expression, however, takes great courage, and in my experience it is rarely possible to achieve it in fullness using the mind alone. The mind must consort with the soul and the body—all three aspects of our being must become involved in a "love triangle"—for the expression and the experience to be complete.

What the dyad denies

Living your life from the place of soul can tell you many things that living your life from the place of mind and body alone cannot. Most of us spend most of our time with our body and our mind, and very little time with our soul. This is not true of everyone, but it is true of the majority of the 6.9 billion people on the earth, if my own observations of life are correct.

The result of this is that we *experience* Individual Life largely from this dyad—the sphere of the body and the sphere of the mind. Not exclusively, but largely. (And, in fact, for some, exclusively.)

The challenge in living Individual Life as a dyad is that we deny ourselves the wisdom of the soul. The soul knows things that the body and the mind do not . . . *cannot.*

When we live our life from our soul, we instantly know the answers to the Four Fundamental Questions of Life: Who we are...where we are... why we came here (to this place called "Earth" and, indeed, to this very moment)...and what we intend to do about that. We choose a State of Being and we step into that. We become a Beingist.

In those moments we see *what the present moment was created for,* and we then use the mind to decide whether we wish to express the beingness we chose to express when the moment was created, or whether we now choose to express something else.

Each moment in life was co-created *for* us *by* the lot of us to allow all of us to express an aspect of divinity. When we peer deeply into each moment, we can see what that moment was designed to allow us to express. We then make up our mind whether we choose to do that. This is called Free Choice. We are not required to express what the moment was designed to allow us to express; we simply have an opportunity to do so.

Should we choose to ignore the opportunity, however, the soul will continue to co-design similar moments and similar opportunities with other souls until we eventually decide to express and experience the Aspect of Divinity that such moments were created and designed to allow us to express and experience.

> Each moment in life was co-created *for* us *by* the lot of us to allow all of us to express an aspect of divinity.

This explains why there is such a thing as Time (we have broken apart EverMoment into segments, so that we have plenty of opportunities to experience the Self fully); and it also explains why some of us live "patterns" in our lives, running into the same kinds of circumstances and situations over and over.

We will continue running into them so long as the soul seeks to experience a particular Aspect of Divinity in a particular way, and the mind chooses not to do so at this time—or not to do so fully.

Yet when we bring the soul into our Individual Life fully, we suddenly see the patterns we have been running—and we see the reasons for them. That is, we see just what the soul is trying to allow the mind to heal, so that the mind can get fully out of its "story" and let the soul do what it came to do.

Once you are ready to truly devote your days and times to what your soul came here to do (as opposed to what your mind is telling you that you are supposed to be doing), you will find your life unimaginably enriched and expanded, filled with meaning and with purpose, and empowered to be expressed through very high States of Being.

And this is not, of course, about ignoring the body and the mind. All three aspects of your being ask for nourishment, and—as in your Collective Life, it is important to keep all three aspects of your Individual Life in balance. So exercise often (or at least a little!), eat well, and watch carefully what you are "feeding" your mind. (What kinds of television programs are you watching? What movies do you see? Do you read a bit in a wonderful book of inspiration each day?)

While the exploration at hand deals primarily with the soul and how to bring it into your everyday life, remember that we are talking about the *triad* here. Soul, mind, and body, yes?

Falling in love with life

Let me back up just a bit and explain how I got to this place—the place from which I am telling you these things.

I have never understood why I was here. From the time I was a child, I never understood that. Who am I? What am I doing here Why is living in this place so hard for so many people so much of the time?

As I looked around me, all I saw was a lot of unhappiness, fear, worry, and apprehension among people. Mind you, this began for me when I was *seven*. I couldn't understand why my Mom and my Dad could not seem to get along, and why there was always fighting in the house.

When I got to school, I couldn't understand why the kids on the playground were always being mean. Later, in high school, I couldn't understand why so many of my classmates seemed to be worried all the time—about grades, about passing or failing, about that Big Test on Friday, about whether He or She was going to like them, about who would go to the prom, and about...yes, about sex, and how to enter into that whole experience without also getting into deep trouble....

All of this was going on all around me and I never understood what all the commotion was about. But as life went on, I began to understand more and more. Bad Things began happening to *me*. I was (and continue to be) amazingly "lucky" much of the time, but even with that, I couldn't seem to get out of the way of some oncoming trains. Life was racing toward me just like everybody else…it just took a little longer for it to get to me, I guess.

But by the time I was 30, I had caught up with all the others in the Struggle Quotient. I had had my share of bad times vs. good times…and I no longer looked at others as if they were from Mars, wondering why they just couldn't "get it," amazed that they couldn't just "be happy."

Now I knew. Now I understood. And now I wondered why *I* just couldn't "get it," and why *I* couldn't just "be happy"!

I could make this story even longer, but I won't. I'll just jump ahead to the day when I began having my conversations with God. I asked God, *What happened? I was so "clear"" as a child. Even as a younger man, I really "had it." What happened?* And God said, in essence, "You lost your way. You stopped believing what you intuitively understood as a child—that life was meant to be *happy*. That you can have anything you want. And, most of all, that it's not about any of this anyway."

Life is not about what we think it's about. I knew that. I knew that as a kid, and I lost it. Now God had come to give that back to me; to bring that awareness back to me. I suddenly realized that 98% of the world's people (myself included) were spending 98% of their time *on things that don't matter;* on things that have nothing to do with anything at all—least of all, the reason that we're *here*.

I realized that life was no longer making any sense—and that it hadn't made any sense for years, since I was young. Then God told me why. "Life will never make any sense to you," God said, "if you're going to continue to consider it from the standpoint of your Mind alone."

Life was being experienced by me as a dyad. I had been moving through it as if I were comprised of just two parts: body and mind. I'd left my soul completely out of the equation.

> Life is not about what we think it's about.

This was not true when I was young. As a child, there was a part of me (which I now, as an adult, call my soul) which *felt* a certain way at a very deep level—a level way below my thinking mind. That place in me felt *good* about life. It felt *love* for all things and for every person. I can remember loving my *pillow*, for heaven sake. And plants in my room. And even the ants that I watched with fascination out in the backyard as a child. I fell in love with the sky and the clouds and the snowflakes and my Red Ryder wagon.

Can you relate to what I am telling you? I'm telling you that *I loved everything around me with the innocence and purity of a child* who didn't see and couldn't understand anything negative—and who couldn't comprehend why *other* people didn't see the world the way *he* did.

> Life will not, it will *never*, make sense to your mind.

Most children run out of this perspective somewhere around age nine. Others perhaps later, in their teens. Believe it or not, I held this perspective until I was about 22. Don't ask me why. I just never let go of it until my mind kicked it out of me, beat it out of me, dragged it out of me One Thought at a Time.

Yet now I'm back where I was as a child. Like Merlin, I somehow seem to be "youthening," rather than aging, in my mind. And I know why that is. It's because I have joined my mind back up with its long-lost buddy...my soul.

How to guarantee you're never happy for long

One of the biggest secrets I was given in *Conversations with God* was this: If you live your life as a function of your body and your mind, without a *daily* awareness of, and collaboration with, your soul, you will *never be continuously happy.* Not for more than a moment here and a moment there. Long-term joy will elude you all the days of your life. Because you are not *here* to experience yourself as a two-part being. You are here to experience the *Totality* of Who You Are.

Life will not, it will *never,* make sense to your mind. But to your mind and your soul *put together*, life will suddenly not only make sense, it will make joy. It will cause you to be very, very happy, peaceful, wonderfully expressed and, sometimes, even fully realized. It will make you fully...how can I say this...fully...*fulfilled.* And this will occur no matter *what* is going on around you.

Yet you must begin to "take in" life, to view life, to embrace life as an experience of the soul, which needs, wants, requires, and lacks nothing; which wishes for nothing; which yearns for nothing; which seeks and reaches for *nothing* except *exactly what is happening Right Here, Right*

Now—knowing that what is happening Right Here, Right Now has been brought TO the soul BY the soul (individually and collectively) so that the Totality of You might decide, announce, express and experience Who You Really Are.

In this knowing you will bless, bless, *bless* your enemies; *pray* for those who persecute you; and live in the rich, quiet, joyful awareness that you possessed when you were seven: that God is on your side, that life was meant to be happy, that it is possible to be happy no matter what is going on (although we are talking about reaching a certain level of mastery here), and that your journey on Earth, and the moments and experiences therein, are but a tiny portion of your everlasting and eternal existence in the blissful and never-ending expression of Divinity through the ages—in you, as you.

Combining experience and wisdom

The idea here, then, is to live into the Soul from the place of your Mind, which is your doorway. This means to experience every moment as a collaboration of the Mind and the Soul.

Most people think of life as something that is happening *to* them. They do not see life as something that is happening *through* them. They experience moments as things that are encountering, rather than things they are co-creating. And they experience Reality as something that is being produced by Life Itself, rather than something that is being produced within their own Being. They have not embraced the idea of *Beingism*.

These misunderstandings of the very nature of things is what creates life for so many people as journeys of difficulty, fear, and unhappiness. Yet

> The secret is to move from the mind to the soul in one's consideration of every moment; to see it from the soul's perspective.

the Master Teacher would tell us that life was never meant to be, and in fact *need not* be, difficult, fearful, or unhappy. And the Master would also tell us that moving from Scenario A to Scenario B can be accomplished without a single thing in your exterior environment or circumstance changing in any way.

The secret is to move from the mind to the soul in one's consideration of every moment; to see it from the soul's perspective; to add *to* the mind's experience the soul's wisdom, awareness, and total knowing. So let's focus in on how to *get* to the soul, in order that we might integrate what the soul knows with what the Mind has experienced regarding any particular moment—and, of course, all of life.

That is the difference, you see. What the mind holds is experience. What the soul holds is knowledge. The mind bases its understanding on the present moment on a very limited storehouse of data, called Prior Experience. The soul, on the other hand, holds the knowledge of All Experience. Put simply, the mind is time limited, the soul is timeless. The mind is temporal, the soul is spiritual. The mind's experience is finite, the soul's knowledge is infinite. Limited experience produces assumptions; unlimited knowledge produces wisdom.

Yes? You see? If you base your decisions and responses and choices on finite resources, your actions will emerge from your experience, which produces assumptions. This will not always be bad, by the way. Sometimes your assumptions are very astute and quite correct. In fact, *much* of the time they are. So your mind serves you well. Its job is to guarantee your physical and emotional survival, and it does that well.

If you base your decisions and responses and choices on infinite resources, your actions will emerge from your knowledge, which produces wisdom. The creates an entirely different expression of life.

Put the mind and the soul *together* and you have a powerful combination.

How to find your way to the soul

The only way to get to the soul is through the mind. The mind is the doorway to the soul and the only way to get to the soul. The big burning question is, how do we use the mind to get to the soul on a consistent and regular basis?

Perhaps the bigger question is, why bother? If we want or need something that cannot be supplied by the body or the mind, why not just go directly to God?

Most people try to do just that. We try to sidestep the soul and go directly to The Boss Upstairs. So we use the mind to go around the soul.

One way we do this is by praying. We pray, "Dear God, please help me. Please help me get this," or "Help me get out of that."

You can get to God that way, but it's the long way around Robin Hood's barn. Using the soul can get us there much faster. This is because when we use the soul to get to God, *we don't have to go anywhere.* And *that* is because the soul *is our direct connection to God.*

It is more than that. That is understating it—or misstating it, actually. The soul *is* God. It is the part of God that resides in us. So when we connect with the soul, we connect with God at the same time.

I've been asked by many people, what are the steps to connecting with the soul? I've thought about it a lot, and I've come up with these...

Step one on the path to the soul

The mind must agree to step out of itself.

Without the mind's agreement, we will not be able to access the soul. The mind will attempt to block everything. Once the mind agrees, then we can move on and start to connect to the soul.

We need to establish that this is no small thing for the mind to agree to. It is not an easy thing for the mind to do because the mind's job is to ensure your survival. See? That is the mind's *function.* What you are asking your mind to do is to let you die. The mind hears your request as a request to let you die.

The mind's job is to ensure your survival by placing before you in every moment all the past data, all the history, all the stories, all the experiences of yourself and others that have come to you by a variety of means to ensure your survival. When you say to the mind, "I need you to step outside of yourself," the mind goes, "Are you kidding me? You want me to step aside here? You want me to get out of your way? That's *suicide.* You cannot get along without me! You understand that?"

The mind has been trained. It has been, in fact, *instructed* never to let go, never to step aside, and never to get out of the way. However, the mind is our friend. It will do what it is instructed by its owner/operator, ultimately. It will obey. The mind is obedient to itself.

So we use the mind to instruct the mind to allow us to be out of our mind. The last thing the mind will say to you is, "Are you out of your mind?" You will say no, not yet, but I need to be. You don't have to say this with words. You can signal the mind with your actions. (I'll describe what this looks like later.) Your mind will say, "Okay, fair enough." Then it will step out of the way.

It does not do that very often in our lives, unless it does. Unless we instruct it to. This is a process of training like training your hair, training your dog, or training anything that needs to be trained. The training of the mind is done with very few words. It's just about closing your eyes and focusing. You'll see what I'm talking about in just a bit.

> You can't get your mind out of the way. That would be like trying to not think of a pink elephant.

It's not about getting the mind out of the way in the classic sense. You can't get your mind out of the way. That would be like trying to not think of a pink elephant. It's impossible to get your mind out of the way. Simply by telling your mind to do that, it is *there*. So the process is…*be there with it.* Don't abandon the mind, or try to shut the mind down. *Be there with it.*

While it is not possible to get your mind out of the way, it *is* possible for your mind to focus away from certain things. This is something that you can do consciously. You simply let the mind step out of itself. I mean, you let it step out of your story, out of your data, out of your history, and out of your experience. You let it go to a place where none of those things exist.

Step two on the path to the soul

In step two—after you have gotten the mind, allowed the mind, to remove its focus from your story, your data, your history, and your experience—tell it to refocus on what you—Big You—now choose to be.

That is, to focus on a state of being. Once you get free of your story and your data, once you get to the space of no-thought, you then choose a state of being. It could be virtually any state of being. This is where the soul resides. The soul resides in the state of Pure Being. This place is broken down into many parts. The soul is being love. It is being compassion. It is being forgiveness. It is being wisdom.

Actually, what it is being is *divine*. It is divinity, residing in *you*. It is you who have broken it down into many parts—so that you could experience it, one part at a time!

Now the mind, of course, will struggle with you as soon as it creates a state of being; decides upon, or focuses upon a state of being. It will bring all that other stuff back in.

For instance, just as an example, let us say that you got to the place where you are feeling "connected"; you're really feeling at one with the moment, the silence, with life itself. You've left your history behind. You're feeling what I would call "happy."

Immediately, because it is trained to do so, the mind will bring you all of your past story, history, data, and current experience around the feeling of happiness. "You cannot be happy! My God, your boss is calling you into his office tomorrow. Your father-in-law is coming over for dinner! Your car broke down and you lost your best ring! How in the hell can you be happy?"

And that's a very good question. Your mind will create a hell for you, then have the nerve to ask you how in the hell you can be happy! Now you can *fake* being happy. You can *try* to be happy. But the mind will come right back in and begin to tell you all that it thinks it knows on the subject of happiness.

Or, let's say you're being "compassionate." That's the State of Being you move into. The mind will say, "You can't be *compassionate*, for heaven's sake! Don't you remember how people treated you when *you* needed compassion? Are you seriously imagining that you can find this now in yourself? Don't be a hypocrite!" If you listen to yourself, you'll hear all the reasons why you cannot rest in the state of being you want to focus on.

> You must cultivate a huge "desire to be" something—whatever that state of being is.

Unless the state of being you choose, that you say you want, you want very, very much. Then the mind will not tell you that you cannot be that. That's the secret. That's the formula. You must cultivate a huge "desire to be" something—whatever that state of being is.

I want to give you a vivid example of what I'm talking about now.

When we really want a beingness badly enough, we can actually get the mind to turn itself off to most of its past data. It's a matter of desire.

> Desire is the key. Pure, honest, deep, unending desire is the key.

The example that I use with an audience is sexual desire. When we are with another person who is totally turning us on, or who we want to turn on, who we want to desire us, to want us, to choose us, and in fact to have us; when we are with a partner or person who we want to want us, we can focus the mind on becoming sensual, sexy, attractive, magnetic, and irresistible. We do it all the time. Sometimes we call this "getting in the mood."

The mind may bring us past data about how to be seductive, how to be sexual, how to be sensual, and how to be magnetic. It will not usually bring us data that stands in our way. Unless we have a serious hang-up about sex, or some previous serious damage or injury (which is another matter altogether—and I'm not making light of that), your mind will not say, "You cannot be that."

Generally speaking, the greater our level of desire to attain a state of beingness, the lower will be your mind's resistance to it. That is actually axiomatic. The mind loves to assist us in having whatever we want, assuming it does not endanger our survival.

Therefore, train the mind to choose a very high level of being, one that is very desirable. One to which the mind will have little if any objection. The mind wants what you want, if it can find no objection. You can find plenty of objection to being, say, happy. But you'll find a lot fewer objections to being sexual. I just use this as an example, to illustrate how the mind works.

So if what you want is a deep, deep sense of connection with your soul, and through that with The Divine, your mind will step out of the way. That is what I meant earlier when I said step out of its own way. It will provide you with that focus and that doorway. It will say, "Over here. The door is over here."

That is why every great spiritual teacher, the great monks, the great spiritualists of past and present, have said the same thing. Desire is the key. Pure, honest, deep, unending desire is the key. That is why it works with people in sexual situations and in certain other situations in life itself. The higher the desire, the lower the mind's resistance. It is axiomatic.

We need to cultivate a hunger for connection. From that hunger and from that deep desire we invite the mind to focus on the soul. Focus first away from your story, your data, by using some mechanisms I am going to share with you. Then, once you've stepped away from your history and your experience, focus through to a state of being. This is the pathway clear to the soul, for the essence of the soul is *beingness*.

I want to say in relative terms, the higher the state of being or the higher the state of beingness upon which you focus, the closer we are to the essence of that beingness. It is the soul itself.

By the way, you should know that we often do all of this subconsciously, spontaneously. We often find ourselves *being* compassionate or *being* courageous and expressing those qualities of being, by going to the soul so *fast* that we don't even know we did it.

I will use two examples. In spontaneous moments in our lives, the mind is totally out of the way. This all happens lightning fast. This is not a half-hour process. This need not be a five-minute process. This need not even be a five-second process. This could be a nanosecond process.

It is the guy who jumps in front of the car and pushes the kid out of the way. It is just a nanosecond process. The mind can get out of the way very quickly when the state of being called for is very high. The state of beingness called for when a man sees the child in the intersection while the child does not see the car coming...the man does not think about it. He moves immediately into *being* courageous, or courage. The mind goes, "Fine," and the body responds. The man pushes the child out of the way, and with luck he gets out of the way himself. If not, he dies. That is how it happens. That is the process. It is a lightning-fast process.

If we choose a high, high state of being, the mind can and will get out of the way—that is, out of our story, your history, etc.—very quickly. So if you want to get in touch with your soul, the state of being that I suggest—and I know this sounds almost blasphemous...it is tough to get people to go there—I suggest holiness.

This is hard for me to even talk about, because it touches so deep. I suggest that people call forth the state of their own holiness. This is not a state that many of us are used to attaining "on command." It can be, however. It can be attained on command. The Christed ones, the Buddha, Mohammad, and the other great masters, both ancient and contemporary, have done precisely and exactly that. It is all that they did.

I once had an interviewer ask me, "How might somebody do that, Neale? How might they tap into that?" I told him, "By calling it forth. Simply say, "I am holy. I *am* what holiness *is*. I am that. Using God's great command, I am that I am. *I am that.*"

It is about focusing on the feeling. It is about getting—after one makes the declaration—getting away from words. Focus on the *feeling* of what it would feel like to be holy, to be a holy person. When I focus on that, my language changes. I swear, my language changes. My demeanor changes. The way I move, the way I walk, and the way I am— my "amness" changes and steps into *beingness*. It is the beingness that I have literally called forth.

It is what I call stepping into being.

I tell you the mind will get out of the way the higher the calling is.

The same thing is true of compassion.

I was in a hospital about ten or twelve years ago visiting my father. There was a guy in the next room. This man was calling out and moaning. He was obviously in pain. The nurse was not coming fast enough. He was in distress. He was moaning, "Oh God, oh, my God, I can't take it." My dad was nowhere near that. He was just lying there feeling perfectly fine.

> I suggest that people call forth the state of their own holiness.

I said hey, I have got to go over there. I have got to go see what's going on next door. He said no. He said son, leave it alone, leave it to the nurses. I said no, I've got to go. I can't let that guy just lie there.

Instantly when I went in there, compassion was called forth. Now listen very carefully to what I just said. I didn't say, "Compassion was called for." I said, "Compassion was called *forth*." This "calling forth" is a process in which the mind, analyzing a situation, *opens an immediate pathway to the soul.* The soul pours forth its Essence—the true Essence of its Being—and that Essence expresses through you, *as* you. This manifests *without effort* because it is, in fact, *who you really are.*

We have all been in situations similar to that, whatever the circumstance, where compassion is called forth. Or patience is called forth. Or forgiveness or kindness or understanding or immense generosity or just plain love…is called forth. This particular version of our Essence just bubbles up. It just comes up in us. We do not think about it. We do not decide, I think I will be compassionate here. The highest callings happen automatically. It is merely a question of whether we will respond to them.

I went in and talked to the guy. I rubbed his forehead. I held his hand. He was an older man about 80 or 85. He was having a terrible time. His meds had run out. His pain had come back. I do not know what was going on with him, but I just talked to him quietly. He did not even care who I was. He did not even care. I could have been a doctor. I could have been a nurse who hadn't put his scrubs on yet. I could have been a psychiatrist who'd been called down from the seventh floor. He had no idea who I was and he did not care. Someone was a witness to his life. That made it all a little easier. Someone was bearing witness…

> The highest callings happen automatically. It is merely a question of whether we will respond to them.

I didn't tell that story to make myself look good. I told it to illustrate something. As I said, we've all had moments like this. We've all experienced "showing up" in life in a very big way, in a very wonderful way. We may not even have seen it as that, but it *was* that, I can tell you, in the life of another.

This is what I mean when I talk about *beingism* as a tool for an individual. This is what I mean when I speak of *beingism* as an engine for an entire society. Imagine what a world we would have if we all simply decided to *be* "compassion." Or to *be* "forgiveness." Or—dare I suggest it?—to *be* "holy."

Step three on the path to the soul

The final step is to simply expand consciousness and awareness.

Expand the ear. I want to say we open the ear. Let those who have ears to hear, listen. We open the ear of consciousness. We become aware of the presence of God in the person of our own soul.

Now if you ask me, How do you do that?, I would say I don't know how to tell you to do that, but *you* will know how to do it. It is just a question of…once you are in that state of being holy, you will just intuitively *know* how to open the ear of consciousness and hear God.

You will simply watch your consciousness expand, like ink on a blotter. (You may have to be in your 60s or 70s to know what either ink or blotters are!) You are not making the ink spread. It is just happening. It is not something you do. It is an allowing. It is the same with your consciousness. You simply allow your consciousness to expand.

It is like on those TV commercials, you know? There was that one where they put down the kitchen tissue—I think they called it *the quicker picker upper*. You watch it pick up the water that was spilled on the table. It's like that. It is just an allowing. It is an absorbing and allowing. You feel your consciousness expand into the silence, into the oneness, and into the experience of your soul.

Beingness produces consciousness. Consciousness produces awareness. Awareness produces perspective. Perspective produces perception. Perception produces belief. Belief produces behavior. Behavior produces experience, and one's whole life changes walking the pathway of the soul.

> Pay attention to what you are aware of.

Then we pay attention to what we are aware of. That I can explain. That is easy to explain. Pay attention to what you are aware of. It is like…have you ever been in a church, in a cemetery, in a movie theater, or any place where you are aware of a lot of things but you're not paying *attention* to anything in particular until somebody says, "Listen! Did you hear that?" You heard it before—that is, your ear received the sound—but *before* you were not paying *attention*.

Now you are. Your ears have not gotten any better than they were three seconds before. The same sound is hitting your eardrums. Only now you're paying attention to what you are aware of. My God, is it a wolf? Is it a lion? Something cracked. I heard it. Somebody…some *thing*…is walking in those woods! I heard a twig snap! Your friend says, "Yeah, that's what I was trying to *tell* you. *Let's get out of here!*"

So in this business of connecting with your soul, you pay attention to what you are aware of. You were always aware, but now you're paying attention. But it's not what your *mind* is aware of, because now you are in the *beingness* of holiness. You pay attention to what *holiness* is aware of. Does that make sense?

Believe you me, holiness, sanctity, is aware of things that you could never even imagine until somebody said, "*Listen.* Let those who have ears to hear, listen." Then you will be aware of what you have always known. You'll begin to feel the wisdom of your soul. That wisdom will become recognizable. That is, you will *re-cognize* it. You will *know it again* to be, in fact, the voice and the wisdom of God.

Some mechanisms you can use

So I've said a lot here. And it all boils down to: The way to get to your soul is not to stop thinking, but rather, to *start* thinking of what your soul is knowing at any particular moment.

The first thing I have to do, as I said, is get my mind to agree. But how to do that? We have to get our mind to get out of its story, to get away from its data. We need a mechanism…some hints on how to pull the mind out of its own history and experience and bring it to Right Now.

There's no right way or wrong way to do this. I don't have the perfect way here. I can only tell you what works for me. So, with that caveat…

I get my mind out of my "story" by pausing as I am moving through any moment or event, taking a deep breath, exhaling it forcefully through my mouth, breathing in again, then closing my eyes and releasing that second breath very slowly, this time gently through my nose, over a period of ten seconds.

During that time I focus my inner attention on the space just above my eyes in the middle of my forehead. Usually this calms me down so much that I want to stay in that place for a longer time. And so, if I can, I do. I take a third deep breath, keep my eyes closed, release that third breath even more slowly than the second, and peer with my Mind's eye deeply into the darkness where I envision my Third Eye.

Now I "look" deeply, deeply, and even more deeply into that velvet jet black darkness…until I make my "connection…"

Usually at that point this is nothing but darkness. If you are seeing images—"thinking thoughts" of something and seeing that in your mind—work to fade those thoughts out, like a "fade to black" on the movie screen. Turn your mind to blankness.

Focusing your inner eye, peer deeply into this darkness. Be looking for nothing in particular, but simply peering deeply, allowing yourself to search for nothing and need nothing.

In my own experience what happens next can often be the appearance of what appears to be a small, flickering blue "flame" or a burst of blue light piercing the darkness. Some people have called this The Blue Pearl.

I find that if I begin thinking about this cognitively—that is, defining it, describing it to myself, trying to give it shape and form or make it "do" something or "mean" something—it disappears immediately. The only way that I can "make it come back" is to pay it no mind.

> Be looking for nothing in particular, but simply peering deeply, allowing yourself to search for nothing and need nothing.

I mean that literally. I have to work hard to turn my mind off and just be with the moment and the experience, without judging it, defining it, or trying to make something happen or figure it out or understand it from my logic center. Once you take your mind off the dancing blue flame, all the while keeping your focus *on* it, without expectation or thought of any kind, the flickering light may reappear. The trick is to keep your mind (that is, your thought process) off it, all the while keeping your focus (that is, your undivided attention) on it.

Thought off, attention on

Can you imagine this dichotomy? This means paying attention to what you are not paying attention to. It is very much like daydreaming. It is like when you're sitting in broad daylight, in the middle of some place of great activity, and you are paying attention to nothing at all—and to everything all at once. You are expecting nothing and requiring nothing and noticing nothing in particular, but you're so *focused* on the "nothing" and the "everything" that someone finally has to snap you out of it (perhaps by literally snapping their fingers), saying, ""Hey! Are you *daydreaming*????"

Usually, one daydreams with one's eyes open. What I'm describing *here* is "daydreaming with your eyes closed." That's as close as I can come to explaining the experience.

Now the dancing blue flame has reappeared. Simply experience it and do not try to define it, measure it, or explain it to yourself in any way. Just...fall into it. The flame may appear to come toward you. It may become larger in your inner field of vision. This is not the flame moving toward you at all, but *you* moving toward *it*; you are moving *into* it, and *inside* of it. And then you become the *experience of It.*

> Usually, one daydreams with one's eyes open. What I'm describing *here* is "daydreaming with your eyes closed."

If you are lucky, you will experience *total immersion* in this light before your mind starts telling you about it and talking to you about it, comparing it to Past Data. If you have even one instant of this mindless immersion, you will have experienced bliss.

This is the bliss of Total Knowing. It is what the soul experiences all the time. It is the total knowing of the Self as One with Everything. It is the soul identifying Itself with the Only Thing There Is.

You cannot "try" for this bliss. If you see the blue flame and begin to anticipate this bliss, the flame will disappear instantly. That's been my experience. Anticipation and/or expectation ends the experience. That's because the experience is happening in EverMoment, and anticipation or expectation *places it into the future, where you are not.*

Hence, the flame seems to "go away."

It has not gone away. *You* have gone away. You have left EverMoment.

This has the same effect on your *inner* eye that closing your *outer* eyes has on your experience of the physical world around you. You quite literally shut it out. You can't see it anymore. It has not left. It is still there. But you can't see it anymore. You've closed your eyes to it.

Mindlessness is achievable by everyone

In my own experience this encounter with bliss comes but once every thousand moments of meditation. Of course, a "moment" is very fast, very quick. It is a nanosecond. Still, the experience of bliss I have described does not come often, even when measured in nanoseconds. Having known it once is both a blessing and, in a sense, a curse, because I am forever wishing for it again. Nevertheless, there are times when I can retreat from the wishing, remove myself from the hope, desert my desires, release my expectations, and place myself totally in the moment, utterly without anticipation of anything in particular. This is the mental state I seek to achieve. It is not easy, but it is possible. And if I achieve it, I have achieved mindlessness.

When I first heard that term—"mindlessness"—it sounded so mysterious to me, so mystical. I thought that it might only be achieved by true spiritual masters. Not so. It is achievable by all of us, by everyone.

Mindlessness is not the emptying of the mind, but the focusing of the mind *away* from the mind. It is about being "out of our mind"— that is, away from your story, your prior data, for a while.

> Mindlessness is not the emptying of the mind, but the focusing of the mind *away* from the mind.

This gets me very close to that blessed place between the Realm of Knowing and the Realm of Experiencing in the Kingdom of God, the Realm of Pure Being. Some have called this place nirvana.

So...if you have managed to find a way to quiet your mind on a regular basis—through sitting meditation; what I call walking meditation; "doing meditation" (doing the dishes can be a wonderful meditation, as can reading, or *writing*, a book); or "stopping meditation" (all of which are described in detail in the book *When Everything Changes, Change Everything*)—you have undertaken what may be the single most important commitment of your entire life: a commitment to your soul, to be *with* your soul, to *meet* your soul, to *hear* and *listen to* and *interact with* your soul.

And...now that you have quieted your mind, you can move into the richness and the depth of your soul, using the three-step process I've described above. So there you have it, a process and the mechanisms to support it. I hope this has been a help to you.

POINTS I HOPE YOU WILL REMEMBER...

• There are not many people who think in terms of the experience and expression of their soul.

• Life invites us to get in touch and stay in touch with our soul.

• Living your life from the place of soul can tell you many things that living your life from the place of mind and body alone cannot.

• Once you are ready to truly devote your days and times to what your soul came here to do, you will find your life unimaginably enriched.

• Life will not, it will *never*, make sense to your mind.

• The secret is to see life from the soul's perspective; to add *to* the mind's experience the soul's wisdom, awareness, and total knowing.

ACTION I HOPE YOU WILL TAKE...

• Develop a method by which you visit your soul every day. That is the only "action step" in this section. It is all you will ever need.

THE MOST VITAL POINT OF ALL

As we close this extraordinary conversation, I hope you will remember its most vital and important point: the problem facing humanity today is a spiritual problem (it has to do with what we *believe*), and it can only be solved by spiritual means. Specifically, our work now is the work of the soul—the soul within each of us, and the Soul of Humanity as a Whole.

That is why I have spent so much time here talking about "beingness." We must decide now who we are as a species, and who we choose to be. Not what we choose to *do*...but who we choose to *be*.

Do we choose to be compassionate? Caring? Loving? Do we choose to live as a Unified Whole, having everything to do with each other, or do we choose to continue living as separate persons, having essentially nothing to do with each other except insofar as we *need* and must *use* each other to ensure our individual happiness and survival?

This is the choice now before us. And it is a larger choice than that. Are we chemical or spiritual? Are we aspects of Divinity or aspects of Physicality? This is the main question. We will answer that question with the living of our lives in the years just ahead, collectively and individually.

It is very important that I remind you of all this, because the second half of my long conversation with you here offers some interesting political and economic proposals. My thought is that these might be considered as foundational concepts for portions of the New Cultural Story that we are all now about to co-author. Yet let us be clear that these proposals were not presented here, nor meant to be viewed, as political or economic strategies, but rather, as spiritual expressions, emerging from a major decision.

That is a decision to produce in our world not a change of circumstance, but a change of consciousness. *That*, and *only* that, is what will allow us all to weather The Storm Before the Calm. And so, then, this call to action. Action unfolding *from*, rather than leading *to*, a State of Being. The action we invite can only materialize from a decision to *be* holy, sacred, divine, caring, compassionate, loving, and One. That action is nothing more (nor *less*) than a simple, gentle, *powerful* conversation between you and all those who you arouse to engage in it with you.

May I please make the point again that this may all not seem like much—it may certainly not seem like world-changing stuff—but in fact, every great movement in history, every major shift of thought and action, has started with a conversation. It's just a matter of how many people we talk to. If we talk to none, nothing will happen. If we talk to many . . . many things can occur.

Thus…The Conversations Movement, inviting us to fill the world with words. Fill newsletters and church bulletins and letters to the editor and pamphlets and flyers and magazine submissions and emails and blogs and texts and tweets and chats and telephone calls and video teleconferences and social network posts with *words*.

Words about a Future Possible. Words about a New Cultural Story to be co-authored by people from all walks of life in every corner of the world. Words about what is happening now on our planet and what we can do to shape it, and not just simply witness it. Words emerging from the Seven Simple Questions.

If you would like to add to the co-authoring of humanity's New Cultural Story, please go now, and go often, to...

www.TheGlobalConversation.com

Let us declare with a single voice the truth of our being: We are all One. And with that declaration as the foundation of our New Cultural Story, let us bring an end, finally, to Separation Theology.

Separation Theology is a theology that insists that we are "over here" and God is "over there." Its doctrine tells us that God separated us from God as punishment for our sins, and that our job now is to get back to

God, which is possible only if God will allow it, which God will do only if we obey God's commands, follow God's laws, and submit to God's will. In short, we must satisfy God's desires.

This Separation Theology has produced a Separation Cosmology (that is, a way of looking at all of life on this planet that includes separation as its basic principle), which, in turn, has produced a Separation Sociology (that is, a way of socializing with each other that encourages us to act as separate beings serving our own separate interests), which, in the end,

> Oneness is not a characteristic of life; life is a characteristic of Oneness.

has produced a Separation Pathology (that is, pathological behaviors of self-destruction, producing suffering, conflict, violence, and death by our own hands).

Only when our Separation Theology is replaced by a Unity Theology will our pathology be healed. We must come to understand that all of life is One.

Oneness is not a characteristic of life; life is a characteristic of Oneness.

The multiplication factor

Should you accept the grandest invitation of all in this book, the invitation to step into beingness as a way of life, you may not touch the whole world, but sociologists tell us that if you are like most of us, you will touch over 10,000 people in your lifetime.

And now, with Internet outreach, that number could easily be multiplied by ten. Imagine, 100,000 people or more, each hearing a simple but powerful message from you. Why, that could start a snowball rolling downhill. And if all of us did it? *It could start an avalanche.* Of such occurrences have landscapes been changed. And it is time now for us to change the Landscape of Our Lives.

Help us, then, if it feels good for you to do so. Help us engage humanity in the Conversation of the Century. Place before the house those Seven Simple Questions. Then stand back and watch the metamorphosis begin.

(METAMORPHOSIS: The process of transformation from an immature form to an adult form in two or more distinct stages; a change of the form or nature of a thing or person into a completely different one, by natural or supernatural means.)

And now, please, one final note: You may discuss anything that you found in this book with me, live, in real time, by Skyping, texting, instant messaging, e-mailing, chatting, posting a video question on the Internet and sending the link to CWGTVmail@gmail.com, or calling me in person on *Talk to Neale,* streamed live on the Internet every Sunday at 1 P.M. Pacific Time at *www.CWG.tv.*

On this one hour weekly web-telecast you may pose questions about the *Conversations with God* material, as well as receive personal spiritual coaching on any matter that may now be challenging you. I hope and trust that you'll call in often so that we can stay connected in a very personal way, and so that we may here, too, engage in the Conversation of the Century.

I am so happy that you have allowed me to begin this conversation with you. We met here by appointment, you and I, joined by our combined destiny. It has been wonderful to travel this path with you. May you have the richest experience of God's forever blessings.

— *Neale*

An invitation from God

My Message is no different from the message that your own heart sings
every time you look into the eyes of another with love.
It is no different from the message that your heart cries out
when you see suffering anywhere.

This is the message that you bring to the world,
and that you would leave with the world,
when you are your True Self.
It is the message that I leave now with you,
that you may remember it once again,
and share it with all those whose lives you touch.

Be kind to each other, and good.
Be kind to yourself, and good, as well.
Understand that these two
do not have to be mutually exclusive.

Be generous with each other, and share.
Be generous with yourself, as well.

Know that only as you share with yourself
can you share with another.
For you cannot give to another
what you do not have.

Be gentle with each other, and true.
Be gentle with yourself, and true, as well.
To thine own self be true, and it follows as the night the day,
thou canst then not be false to any man.

Remember always that betrayal of yourself
in order not to betray another
is betrayal nonetheless.
It is the highest betrayal.

Remember always that love is freedom.
You need no other word to define it.
You need no other thought to comprehend it.
You need no other action to express it.

Your search for the true definition of love is over.
Now the only question will be whether you can give this gift of love
to yourself and to another, even as I have given it to you.

All systems, agreements, decisions, and choices
that express freedom express God.
For God *is* freedom, and freedom is love, expressed.

Remember always that yours is a world of Illusion,
that nothing you see is real, and that you may use The Illusion
to bring you a grand experience of the Ultimate Reality.
Indeed, that is what you have come here to do.

You are living in a dream of your own creation.
Let it be the dream of a lifetime, for *that is exactly what it is.*

Dream of a world in which the God and Goddess in you is never denied,
and in which you never again deny the God and the Goddess in another.
Let your greeting, both now and forevermore, be *Namaste.*
Dream of a world in which love is the answer to every question, the solution to
every problem, the response to every situation, the experience in every moment.

Dream of a world in which Life, and that which supports Life, is the highest value,
receives the highest honor, and has its highest expression.

Dream of a world in which freedom becomes the highest expression of life,
in which no one who claims to love another seeks to restrict another, and in which
all are allowed to express the glory of their being in measure full and true.

Dream of a world in which equal opportunity is granted to all,
and equal resources are available to all, and equal dignity is accorded to all,
so that all may experience equally the unequalled wonder of Life.

Dream of a world in which judgment is never again visited by one upon another,
in which conditions are never again laid down before love is offered,
and in which fear is never again seen as a means of respect.

Dream of a world in which differences do not produce divisions,
individual expression does not produce separation,
and the greatness of The Whole is reflected in the greatness of Its Parts.

Dream of a world in which there is always enough, in which the simple gift of sharing leads to that awareness—and creates it, and in which every action supports it.

Dream of a world in which suffering is never again ignored, in which intolerance is
never again expressed, and in which hatred is never again experienced by anyone.

Dream of a world in which ego is relinquished,
in which superiority is abolished, and in which ignorance is eliminated
from everyone's reality, reduced to the Illusion that it is.

Dream of a world in which mistakes lead not to shame,
regrets lead not to guilt, and judgment leads not to condemnation.

Dream of these things, and more.
Do you choose them?
Then *dream them into being.*
With the might of your dreams,
end the nightmare of your imagined reality.

You can choose this.
Or … you can choose The Illusion.

Which do you choose?

— from
Communion with God

One possible response from Humankind . . .

With a good conscience our only sure reward, with history the final judge of our deeds, let us go forth to lead the land we love, asking His blessing and His help, but knowing that here on earth, God's work must truly be our own.

—the final words
of the inaugural
address of
John F. Kennedy

Contact Points

www.TheGlobalConversation.com

www.CWG.tv

www.nealedonaldwalsch.com

———————————

I am so very impressed with all that I see going on around me now as humanity's Cultural Creatives (you among them) begin to move swiftly to assist our species in recreating itself anew in the next grandest version of itself.

There are many, many such undertakings now manifesting around the world, and I want to point you to the Other Initiatives and Resources tab on the website at TheGlobalConversation.com, where you will find some wonderful information on these programs and projects.

Life is inviting us now to all work together—to "think together and link together," as I like to put it—and so I hope that you will check out this tab and "link up" with whatever outreach you find there with which you feel to be in harmony.